Ethical Problems and Genetics Practice

Ethical Problems and Genetics Practice provides a rich, case-based account of the ethical issues arising in the genetics clinic and laboratory. By analysing a wide range of evocative and often arresting cases from practice, Michael Parker provides a compelling insight into the complex moral world of the contemporary genetics professional and the challenges they face in the care of patients and their families. This book is essential reading for anyone interested in the ethical issues arising in everyday genetics practice. *Ethical Problems and Genetics Practice* is also a sustained engagement with the relationships between bioethics and social science. In proposing and exemplifying a new approach to bioethics, it makes a significant contribution to debates on methods and interdisciplinarity and will therefore also appeal to all those concerned with theoretical and methodological approaches to bioethics and social science.

MICHAEL PARKER is Professor of Bioethics and Director of the Ethox Centre at the University of Oxford, where his research focuses on the ethical implications of the clinical use of genetics and on the ethical aspects of collaborative global health research.

Cambridge Bioethics and Law

This series of books was founded by Cambridge University Press with Alexander McCall Smith as its first editor in 2003. It focuses on the law's complex and troubled relationship with medicine across both the developed and the developing world. In the past twenty years, we have seen in many countries increasing resort to the courts by dissatisfied patients and a growing use of the courts to attempt to resolve intractable ethical dilemmas. At the same time, legislatures across the world have struggled to address the questions posed by both the successes and the failures of modern medicine, while international organisations such as the WHO and UNESCO now regularly address issues of medical law.

It follows that we would expect ethical and policy questions to be integral to the analysis of the legal issues discussed in this series. The series responds to the high profile of medical law in universities, in legal and medical practice, as well as in public and political affairs. We seek to reflect the evidence that many major health-related policy debates in the UK, Europe and the international community over the past two decades have involved a strong medical law dimension. With that in mind, we seek to address how legal analysis might have a trans-jurisdictional and international relevance. Organ retention, embryonic stem cell research, physician-assisted suicide and the allocation of resources to fund health care are but a few examples among many. The emphasis of this series is thus on matters of public concern and/or practical significance. We look for books that could make a difference to the development of medical law and enhance the role of medico-legal debate in policy circles. That is not to say that we lack interest in the important theoretical dimensions of the subject, but we aim to ensure that theoretical debate is grounded in the realities of how the law does and should interact with medicine and health care.

Series Editors
Professor Margaret Brazier, *University of Manchester*
Professor Graeme Laurie, *University of Edinburgh*
Professor Richard Ashcroft, *Queen Mary, University of London*
Professor Eric M. Meslin, *Indiana University*

Marcus Radetzki, Marian Radetzki, Niklas Juth
Genes and Insurance: Ethical, Legal and Economic Issues

Ruth Macklin
Double Standards in Medical Research in Developing Countries

Donna Dickenson
Property in the Body: Feminist Perspectives

Matti Häyry, Ruth Chadwick, Vilhjálmur Árnason, Gardar Árnason
The Ethics and Governance of Human Genetic Databases: European Perspectives

Ethical Problems and Genetics Practice

Michael Parker

The Ethox Centre, University of Oxford

CAMBRIDGE
UNIVERSITY PRESS

CAMBRIDGE UNIVERSITY PRESS
Cambridge, New York, Melbourne, Madrid, Cape Town,
Singapore, São Paulo, Delhi, Mexico City

Cambridge University Press
The Edinburgh Building, Cambridge CB2 8RU, UK

Published in the United States of America by Cambridge University Press,
New York

www.cambridge.org
Information on this title: www.cambridge.org/9781107020801

First published 2012

Printed in the United Kingdom at the University Press, Cambridge

A catalogue record for this publication is available from the British Library

ISBN 978-1-107-02080-1 Hardback

Contents

Acknowledgements

This book has taken a long time to write and far too many people have influenced the writing of it and the ideas in it for me to be able to mention them all individually by name. I would, however, like to say thank you to at least some of the people who have made this book possible.

For the past ten years or so, since our first monthly case discussion, which I describe in Chapter 1, the team at the Oxford Regional Genetics Service at the Churchill Hospital have generously welcomed me as a member of their group. I would like to thank all of the clinical geneticists, genetic counsellors and laboratory staff who have worked at the Churchill over this period including those of you who have since gone on to work elsewhere. Without your warmth, openness, generosity and spirit of critical reflection I would never have written this book. For obvious reasons, I have been very careful not to use any cases presented or discussed in Oxford. Nevertheless, this book owes a lot to the discussions we have had and to all the things I have learnt in my time with you.

Without doubt, the biggest single influence on the content of this book has been the Genethics Club. It is not really necessary or appropriate for me to say anything very much about it here because the book as a whole is itself my attempt to make sense of why and how the Genethics Club works and why it has had such enduring appeal. Nevertheless, one of the main reasons for this has clearly been the enthusiasm and commitment of everyone who has attended and in particular the willingness of those who have presented cases to open up their work to discussion and critical reflection with others in this forum. I would like to take this opportunity to thank everyone who has ever attended the Genethics Club. Never has it been truer for an author to say that his book would not have been possible without you.

The Genethics Club was not my idea alone. Building on the work I was doing at the Oxford Regional Genetics Service with Anneke Lucassen, the idea for the club was initially conceived by Angus Clarke, Tara Clancy, Anneke and myself and further developed by a group of genetics professionals from around the United Kingdom who we invited to attend a symposium on ethical issues in clinical genetics in Oxford in 2000. In practice, the success of the Genethics Club has been largely due to the enthusiasm and enduring commitment of Angus, Tara and Anneke. Working with them on this continues to be a real pleasure and I'm hoping we've got a few more years in us yet.

Over the years, I have also discussed the topics explored in this book with many academic friends and colleagues outside of the world of genetics. Of particular value to me have been conversations with social scientists including Mary Boulton, Mary Dixon-Woods, Mikey Dunn, Ray Fitzpatrick, Nina Hallowell, Cate Heeney, Annemarie Mol, Bob Simpson, Margaret Sleeboom-Faulkner, Mariam Fraser, Marilyn Strathern and Steve Woolgar. These conversations have been of special importance because one of my aims in this book and in the work leading up to it has been to try to find a way of doing bioethics which takes the methodological and theoretical concerns of both philosophy and the social sciences seriously. To the extent that this has been successful it is due in large measure to the encouragement of and discussion with the people above. The book's failings in this regard are as in all others of course my own.

I have also benefitted hugely from discussion of the ideas in this book with colleagues at the Ethox Centre over a number of years. Ethox is a really stimulating place to work. The collegiate atmosphere and supportive critical research culture at the Centre have been key to the writing of this book and important sources of inspiration for me in my other work. There isn't space to mention everyone in the centre individually by name here but I am truly grateful to everyone in the Ethox team for their support with this book and with the development of the Centre and its work.

Several people have been kind enough to read and make helpful comments on sections of the book in draft form. Richard Ashcroft, Tara Clancy, Mikey Dunn, Tony Hope, Anneke Lucassen and Mark Sheehan each read and commented on several chapters and Mariam Fraser read everything a number of times. Stefan Baumrin, Nathan Case, Kurt and Rochelle Hirschhorn and Rosamond Rhodes all gave me very helpful comments and suggestions on the 'moral craft' chapter when I presented it at the Mount Sinai Medical School in New York in Spring 2011.

Although I have already mentioned her several times above, I would like to take this opportunity to say a special thank you to Anneke Lucassen. Anneke has been a wonderfully supportive friend and colleague to me over the years we have known each other. Thinking and talking together about the kinds of issues discussed in this book and writing papers as a way of thinking these things through has been and continues to be a great pleasure for me.

I would like to thank Elsevier for giving me permission to include Chapter 7 which is based on my paper, 'Ethnography/ethics' (2007) 65 *Social Science and Medicine*, 2248–2259. I would also like to thank the Wellcome Trust for providing us with a symposium grant (SYM/3/99) to support the first meeting of the Genethics Club, and for establishing an archive of the papers relating to the Genethics Club at the Wellcome Collection in London. Thanks to Jessica Myring for the family pedigree diagram that appears in Chapter 2 and a very special thanks to Tim Harris for permission to use one of his beautiful paintings for the image on the cover.

Finally, my partner Mariam Fraser has discussed all of the ideas in this book with me and the whole way I see things is different because of our time together.

1   Introduction

I've got a young patient with a family history of Huntington's Disease who wants to have a test to see whether she is going to be affected by the disease as she gets older. She is worried because she knows that her paternal grandmother has it. During counselling my patient disclosed that she is an identical twin. She says that her twin sister is not aware of the family history and says that she does not want her sister to know because she doesn't think that she could cope with this knowledge, particularly because the disease is untreatable. When I told her that I was reluctant to do the test on her without discussing it with her sister – because the fact that they are identical twins means that the test would also be a test on her twin – she said that she didn't want her sister to be involved. To reassure me, she promised that whatever the test result she would not disclose this. The other problem I have got is that in addition to being a test on her twin the test, if positive, would also be test on her father who, she says, also does not know that she has come in for testing. I've tried to encourage her to talk to her sister and father about the test but she says that she's not able to do this. I feel that I have got a duty of care to my patient, but I'm also worried about her sister and father even though I have never met them.

A woman who is trying to get pregnant was recently referred to me because she is a member of a family with a history of a serious X-linked disorder. Her cousin is affected. My patient is interested in using preimplantation genetic diagnosis (PGD) to ensure that she doesn't have an affected baby. We didn't have any information about the mutation in the family so we had to carry out a linkage study to assess her risk. This meant looking at samples from a number of other family members. We were talking about a generation of people in their fifties and over. They were all very happy to provide blood samples. When we tested the samples, however, it became clear that one of them had no genetic markers in common with anyone else in the family, suggesting possible adoption, and another showed non-paternity. These results mean that my patient is not at risk of the condition. What should we do? These events were a long time in the past. Is it acceptable to simply tell my patient that there is no risk of the disease in this part of the family or does she need to know that she is adopted?

> The person concerned is now deceased so it is not possible to go back to them to ask for their consent to share this information. So, we are just left with this and not knowing how to deal with it.

As these two stories show, genetic testing can sometimes tell us more about ourselves and about our relationships with the people around us than we expect, and perhaps, in some cases, more than we really want to know. The stories also show that genetic testing can sometimes end up telling us rather *less* than we might have wanted to know because of the ways that decisions about access to genetic testing and the distribution of the results of such testing are mediated by the complexities of the relationships we have with those around us, such as our family members, and by the policies and practices of the health care institutions and genetics professionals who are – even in the era of the Internet and direct-to-consumer genetic testing – most often the gatekeepers of such testing and advice. What we come to know about ourselves and about our relationships through genetic testing depends to an important degree upon the decisions and values of our relatives and the ways in which they conceive of their relationships with us, and upon the views of the genetics professionals who offer or refuse to offer such tests, and the guidelines by which their practice is informed.

What these stories also reveal is that there is a *co-productive* relationship between genetic testing and decisions about whether or not to make it available, and the nature of our relationships with relatives and reproductive partners. Our knowledge about and understanding of our relationships with others, and consequently the very nature of those relationships themselves, has the potential to be shaped in significant ways by practice in genetics. This is increasingly likely to be the case in the future as genetics inevitably becomes more a part of mainstream medicine and as genetic testing in one form or another becomes a more pervasive feature of life outside the clinic.[1] In both of the stories above, for example, genetic testing and the sharing of the information resulting from such tests (or the refusal to do so) has the potential to radically alter the relationships between those who have been or wish to be tested and others in their families. Just as these stories show that genetic testing can create new ways – or maintain old ways – of being related, they also show that such influences can work in the opposite direction – that is, they help us to see how the particularities and complexities of the ways in which we are related to those around us have the potential to make a difference to the development, use, availability and

---

[1] PFG Foundation, *Genetics and Mainstream Medicine: Service Development and Integration* (Cambridge: PFG Foundation, 2011).

understanding of genetic technologies and of the genetic information produced by them. A good example of this is the way in which the twin's understanding of the nature of her relationships with her sister and her father in the first story above informs her decision not to include them in her deliberations about testing. Another is the way in which the genetics professional in the second case worries – and the very fact that she does worry – about the implications of information about adoption and 'non-paternity' for her patient's wellbeing. Seen from this angle, what these stories serve to highlight is that just as genetics has the potential to change the nature of our relationships with the people around us, the ways in which we are related also have the potential to change the practice of genetics. The day-to-day practice of genetics, the translation of new genetic technologies, and the transformation of human relationships are interwoven in complex and dynamic ways.

Because of their significance for people's lives and for the kinds of relationships they have with the people around them, many of the questions posed by the use of genetics inevitably have a moral or ethical aspect. Sometimes these are questions which people struggle with as patients or as family members. In the first story above, for example, the twin wrestles with the tensions between her desire for the Huntington's test, her recognition that the results of the test will be of relevance to her sister, and her concern about the potential harms that might happen to her sister if the results were to turn out to be positive. Does she – she wonders – have an obligation to talk to her sister about the test? If so, might this nevertheless be outweighed by concerns about her sister's wellbeing or by her own right to gain access to health care without the requirement to seek permission from or take on responsibility for, her relatives? In addition to the moral difficulties experienced by patients and their families, the potential uses of genetics and of the information generated by genetic tests can also present difficult ethical questions for genetics professionals – for the counsellors, doctors and laboratory staff who work in clinical genetics. In many cases, such as in the first story above, the ethical challenges are to some extent shared by the patient and the genetics professional. Here, in addition to the worries confronting the patient herself, the genetics professional is also faced with a tension between her duty to do the best for her patient and her sense that she has responsibilities for the wider family. There are also some situations in which genetics professionals face difficult ethical challenges of which patients may be completely unaware. In the second story, for example, to ask the patient about whether she would want to know that she was adopted would probably be to reveal to her that she is. The question of whether or not to disclose this information is something the genetics professional must wrestle with alone, or with the help of her colleagues.

In the stories above, genetics professionals are called upon to make difficult moral decisions with the potential to impact upon the social as well as the medical lives of their patients and with significant implications for the distribution and use of genetic technologies and information. This reflects the key role genetics professionals play at the interface between technology, science, health care practice and contemporary human relations. The moral complexities of this role are striking both in their particularities and in their scope. For not only does the genetics professional deal with individually difficult cases with morally significant implications for the lives of specific patients and their families, the fact that she and her colleagues encounter such problems on a day-to-day basis, as a profession, means that in her practice the genetics professional plays an important role both in the development and implementation of genetic technologies and in the forming, sustaining and transformation of human relationships more broadly.

There has been extensive discussion of the implications of genetics and of genomics in the media and in the academic bioethics and social science literature. Much of this has focused on the implications of developments in genetics for patients and their families. These debates are familiar, if not over-familiar. Despite this, there is very little on the relationships between developments in genetics and the contexts into which they are being or may be translated. This is the domain of the genetics professional: a dynamic and complex space of moral commitments and material practices in which genetic tests are carried out, and their implications unravelled, in real and material ways with patients and their families over time. This book aims to provide a rich account of the moral world of the contemporary genetics professional at a key moment in its development.

The work informing this book has its origins in three conversations I had with clinical geneticists in 1999 and 2000. The first of these was with Anneke Lucassen at Oxford in the summer of 1999 shortly after I had started a new post at the Ethox Centre.[2] Anneke was a consultant geneticist at the Regional Genetics Unit in Oxford at that time[3] and our conversation started because she was attending a 'masterclass' in medical ethics that was being run by the Ethox Centre and on which I was a tutor. The masterclass format combined seminars on various topics in

---

[2] The Ethox Centre is a multidisciplinary bioethics research centre in the University of Oxford (www.ethox.ox.ac.uk).

[3] Anneke is now Professor of Clinical Genetics at Southampton University.

medical ethics with an opportunity for participants to work on a piece of ethics writing with one-to-one tutorial support. Anneke, who had come to the masterclass because of her interest in medical ethics, had brought with her a couple of cases from her own practice which she had found ethically challenging and which she wanted to write up. In these cases, genetic tests had identified, as an 'incidental finding', misattributed paternity. As we worked on developing the paper over the course of the week, Anneke and I had a number of fascinating discussions about the ethical aspects of day-to-day practice in clinical genetics.[4] These were of interest to me both in themselves and for two further reasons. First, I had a long-standing fascination with the importance of relationships in ethics and, in particular, with the relationships between individuals and families[5] and the cases that Anneke and I were discussing seemed to offer new and productive ways of thinking about this issue. Second, and more prosaically, my new position at Oxford required me to spend the equivalent of one day a week providing clinical ethics support to health professionals in the local hospital. As our conversations developed, the regional clinical genetics service – where Anneke worked – began to emerge as an ideal setting in which to begin this work.[6] Anneke discussed this possibility with the clinical team, who proposed that I give a presentation at one of their weekly case conferences. This was to be the second conversation I had that would lead to the writing of this book.

Over the course of the next four weeks, in order to prepare for the talk, I built on my earlier work on genetics[7] by reading as much as I could of the bioethics literature and by talking to people, including Anneke, who I knew had worked in this area. My presentation to the clinical genetics team would be the first time I had met health professionals since my arrival in Oxford and I wanted to make sure that I did a good job. I wanted the presentation to be interesting, to emphasise the importance of the ethical dimensions of genetics and, hopefully, to convince the

---

[4] This paper was published in *The Lancet* as: A. Lucassen and M. Parker 'Revealing false paternity: some ethical considerations' (2001) 357 *The Lancet*, 1033–1035.

[5] This interest was in large part formed by my work, over the course of the earlier decade, with young homeless teenagers and families in conflict. See for example: M. Parker, 'Children who run: ethics and homelessness', in B. Almond, *Introducing Applied Ethics* (Oxford: Blackwell, 1995), pp. 58–70.

[6] I later provided clinical ethics support in a number of other settings in the hospital, including adult and neonatal intensive care and emergency medicine.

[7] M. Parker and D. Dickenson, *The Cambridge Medical Ethics Workbook* (Cambridge University Press, 2001); M. Parker, R. Williamson and J. Savulescu, *Ethical Issues in Genetics Research: An Introduction for Members of Australian Human Research Ethics Committees* (Melbourne: Cooperative Research Centre for the Discovery of Genes for Common Human Diseases, 2003).

genetics team that they might benefit from a regular meeting with an 'ethicist'. On the morning of the presentation, one of the senior consultants from the genetics unit arrived at my office to accompany me on the short walk over to the clinic. As we set off across the car park on a lovely sunny day, she told me how much the team were looking forward to the session. She said that ethical issues were, increasingly, a major part of their practice and that the geneticists worried about this a lot. This made me feel a bit more confident about my talk. She then mentioned, as an aside, that the team had once before invited someone to 'give a talk on ethics' and 'that', she added portentously, 'was exactly what he had done'. Without realising or intending its impact on me, she finished by saying that they had never invited him back.

It was clear to me that I had seriously misjudged the nature of the event but I had no idea what the alternatives might be. As we continued our walk, I tried to decide what to do. Should I give my prepared talk as planned, making it as interesting as possible but accepting from the outset that this was not likely to lead to an invitation to return? Or should I try to come up with a different kind of improvised approach in the five minutes available to me? In the end, I decided that the only sensible thing to do was to introduce myself, say something about the work I had been doing with Anneke on the difficulties of dealing with unexpected information, and then to ask them what they themselves considered to be the most important ethical issues in their everyday practice.

We arrived at the meeting a few minutes early, as a clinical case discussion involving a twin who had requested a test for Huntington's Disease was coming to a close. The meeting room was no larger than the average living room. Its walls were covered by shelves of cardboard boxes which contained, I assumed, medical records. At its centre was a large table surrounded by approximately ten people, and behind these, seated against the walls, were about another twenty. As I listened to the discussion of the case, it became clear that the people in the room came from a variety of different backgrounds: genetic counsellors, nurses, laboratory staff, consultants and registrars. There was even a medical anthropologist, sitting in the corner, quietly taking notes. When it came to my turn to speak I introduced myself, mentioned my work with Anneke, and went on to say something – I can't remember what – about the ethical aspects of the case they had just been discussing in their case conference. I concluded by enquiring whether these kinds of issues arose very often in their practice. In this way, my second conversation began.

After asking this question, an hour of heated discussion ensued in which one person after another described difficult situations they had been involved in, only to be followed by another who agreed on the importance of the issue, but who took a different view about what should be done and who could support their position with another case from their own experience. Although I had said no more than three or four sentences during this discussion, it was agreed at the end of the session that the team's agenda would include a regular slot dedicated to the discussion of ethics, that I would facilitate this, and that someone in the genetics unit would work with the team and with me to identify cases for each monthly meeting. The first of these meetings took place in 1999 and they have taken place more or less every month since. The approach that I had unintentionally adopted, in which I facilitated the discussion rather than led it, had worked very well and the event served as a model for much of the work I have done in bioethics ever since.

The third and final conversation, and perhaps the most significant with regard to the writing of this book, also took place in Oxford. In Spring 2001, Angus Clarke, Tara Clancy, Anneke Lucassen and I obtained a grant to bring together a small number of genetics professionals from across the United Kingdom to talk about the ethical issues arising in clinical genetics.[8] With the consent of those present, this meeting was taped and transcribed. When I looked back at the transcript as I prepared to write this introduction, I was struck by the similarities between the discussion at that workshop and the one in the clinical genetics unit which I have described above. The plan had been that we would introduce the aims of the meeting at the start of the day and then follow an agenda organised around a number of key issues which Angus, Anneke, Tara and I had identified in advance as important. What happened was very different. In my role as the facilitator of the meeting, I began by suggesting that we introduce ourselves and say something about the kinds of ethical issues that we thought were important in genetics practice. Although there were no more than twenty people in the room, it took the entire length of the meeting (about four hours) to complete these 'introductions'. As each person set out what they thought were the interesting issues, and gave cases as examples, others joined in and gave their own, sometimes contrasting, examples, going on to provide richer and richer accounts of the nature of the problems they were facing and the different ways in which these problems might arise.

We never got on to the agenda. We did, however, allocate time at the end of the day to thinking about how some of these issues might be addressed. One of the most important ideas to come out of that discussion was a suggestion that a regular national ethics forum should be

8 This symposium was funded by a grant from the Wellcome Trust (SYM/3/99).

established at which anyone working in clinical genetics could present and discuss cases with the aim of sharing experiences and potentially working towards models of good practice. The idea for the format had its origins in a national forum which had already been successful in relation to the clinical aspects of practice – the Dysmorphology Club.[9] Angus Clarke, Tara Clancy, Fiona Douglas, Anneke Lucassen and I agreed to take on the task of organising the forum, and the first meeting of what came to be known as the 'Genethics Club' took place later in the same year.

Our aim in establishing the Genethics Club was to provide a regular forum at which anyone working in clinical genetics in the United Kingdom could present and discuss ethical issues arising in their practice. We knew from our experience and from the discussions at the meeting described above that there was significant diversity of experience across the different clinical genetics units in the United Kingdom and our idea was that the Genethics Club should be both a space in which people could feel comfortable discussing the difficulties they faced and an opportunity to work towards shared models of good practice through its encouragement of communication between regional units.

At the time of writing, the Genethics Club has met thirty times, being attended on average by about thirty people (ranging from a low of twenty at one meeting to sixty-five at another). Because the meetings are always attended by a significant number of new people, they begin with a welcome and an introduction from either myself or Anneke about the origins and purpose of the Genethics Club. As part of this introduction, one of us – usually me – outlines the Genethics Club's approach to confidentiality. The policy is straightforward. Those who present cases are asked to ensure that they are anonymised. This is important because although, if the meeting is to function effectively, the issues and cases discussed need to be real, the meetings are usually attended by people such as myself who are either not directly involved in the care of the patients or are not health professionals at all. Given the nature of clinical genetics in a relatively small country, there is also sometimes the possibility that the families discussed may be recognisable to clinicians from other regional centres. For this reason, the general rule we have adopted is that when genetics professionals go back to their clinical teams and discuss the issues that were raised at the Genethics Club, this should be done in a way which ensures that as far as possible

---

[9] For more information, see www.clingensoc.org/Dysmo/index.htm (accessed 1 August 2011).

the families are not recognisable to their colleagues. Following these introductory remarks, the time available for the day is divided up to ensure there is space available for discussion of all the cases that have been brought along. On average about ten formal case presentations are made at each meeting.

It is important to point out that, as the story above of the origin and development of the Genethics Club illustrates, this is very much a book about ethics and genetics *in the Genethics Club*, and as encountered by the genetics professionals who have participated in the Genethics Club, rather than a book about 'genetics'. Nevertheless, in providing a space – one might call it a laboratory – for ethics, the Genethics Club has arguably *changed* genetics (genetics as practice) in significant respects.[10] The story above also serves to highlight the significance of my own role in, and to some extent outside of, the Genethics Club. When asked, I have sometimes described this role as follows:

My role in the Genethics Club is essentially concerned with facilitating the discussion in a way which doesn't interfere too much but is attentive to the morally significant features of the cases presented and of the subsequent discussion. I organise the space and lunches, etc., and, inevitably, I've done a certain amount of behind-the-scenes work to encourage people to bring cases along. But primarily my role has been to ensure that anyone who wants to speak has the opportunity to do so and that as many voices as possible are heard.

Essentially, this has been my role. But, particularly as I have gained experience over time, my participation in the discussion has been more active than this. For example, I have sometimes used my experience of involvement in the regional genetics service in Oxford, my reading of the literature and my experience of previous Genethics Club meetings, to challenge positions taken when it has seemed to me that a too-easy consensus has been reached, to introduce issues that I think have been neglected, or to remind those present of the views taken in relation to similar cases in previous meetings. These aspects of my role have been made possible at least in part by the fact that, since the first meeting of the Genethics Club, I have kept reasonably detailed notes of the cases presented and, as much as has been compatible with my role as facilitator, set down the range of positions taken in the subsequent discussion. On four or five occasions, the group has agreed to record the Genethics Club meetings as a way of preserving the debate, identifying possible topics for invited plenary presentations and capturing enduring themes

---

[10] I develop this point further in Chapter 6.

and issues for further, future discussion. In the chapters that follow, I have included short extracts from these notes and transcripts.[11]

But, who are the 'genetics professionals' who attend the Genethics Club? Clinical genetics services in the United Kingdom are provided through twenty-three Regional Genetics Centres, which can cover very large populations – the centre in Manchester, for example, serves a population of about five million people.[12] Services are provided through the centres themselves, through outreach clinics in District General Hospitals or on hospital wards, and – sometimes – through visits to patients' homes. The majority of genetics professionals who attend the Genethics Club work in these regional centres. Like those in genetics services in many other countries, the staff members in Regional Genetics Centres fall, broadly speaking, into three main categories. *Clinical Geneticists* are medical doctors (physicians) who have undergone specialty training in genetics after general medical training (or, sometimes after specialty training in a related field such as paediatrics). This means that some of the clinical geneticists in the regional genetics centre will be fully trained consultants and others will be junior doctors in training. The role of the clinical geneticist is diagnosis, risk estimation and the management and support of patients and families affected by or at risk of inherited conditions. *Genetic Counsellors*, who are also sometimes referred to as specialist genetic nurses, genetic associates or genetic co-workers, will either have completed a Masters in Genetic Counselling or have undergone several years postgraduate professional training in counselling and some training in genetics and will also be a qualified health professional – most often a nurse. The role of the genetic counsellor is to help individual patients and their families to understand information about the nature of the genetic condition, appreciate the inheritance pattern and risk of recurrence, understand the options available, make decisions appropriate to their personal and family situation, and make the best possible adjustment to the disorder or risk.[13] The clinical geneticists and genetic counsellors at the twenty-three regional clinical genetics centres provide services related to a range of types of inherited disorders including neuromuscular conditions, eye diseases, neuropsychiatry, adult and paediatric endocrinology, cardiac, deafness, dysmorphology, infertility, and a range of other adult and

[11] I return to discussion of my role in the Genethics Club, and to my analysis of the Genethics Club as an 'ethico-ethnographic' research technique in Chapter 7.
[12] PFG Foundation, *Genetics and Mainstream Medicine*.
[13] Association of Genetic Nurses and Counsellors website www.agnc.org.uk/howtobecomeaGC.htm (accessed 24 July 2011).

common diseases. In most regional centres there will usually be a specific group of clinical geneticists and genetic counsellors who specialise in cancer and working with patients and families affected by or at risk of inherited cancers and with the identification and management of individuals at risk of developing cancer because of their family history.

In addition to clinical geneticists and genetic counsellors, the Genethics Club is also attended by *Clinical Scientists* from the NHS genetics laboratories associated with the regional genetics centres. These genetic laboratories can be very large. The laboratories in Manchester and Birmingham, for example, have staff teams of 200 and 160 respectively and carry out a high volume of genetic tests. In the year 2009–10 the laboratory in Birmingham processed 48,000 samples. These samples were roughly evenly divided between cytogenetics (20,000 samples) and molecular diagnostic testing (28,000 samples).[14] The kinds of testing services offered by these laboratories include prenatal testing, postnatal testing, e.g. for developmental disorders, specific tests for single gene disorders and syndromes, and oncology services, e.g. cancer diagnosis and monitoring of disease status.

The clinical geneticists, genetic counsellors and laboratory staff in regional genetics centres and their associated laboratories work in collaboration with a range of specialties outside of genetics. These include obstetrics, paediatrics, neurology, cardiology and oncology/cancer surgeons. Regional genetics centres also, inevitably, because of their contact with patients and their wider families, work closely with general practitioners (family doctors). In addition to the members of regional genetics centres, the Genethics Club is, even if to a lesser extent, attended by members of these other groups involved in the clinical use of genetics.[15]

Against this background, this book aims to provide an account of the moral world of the genetics professional through an exploration of how the moral commitments underpinning ideas of 'good practice' in contemporary clinical genetics are transformed into ethical problems. Taking as its starting point the genetics professional's commitment to the care of the patient in the family, Chapter 2 investigates how ethical problems are created for genetics professionals by the ways in which the construction and verification of the family

---

[14] Cytogenetics concerns the analysis of structure and function of chromosomes. Molecular diagnostic testing, by contrast, uses a variety of techniques to identify genetic variation at the molecular level including mutation analysis for inherited disorders.

[15] This seems likely to increase with the mainstreaming of genetics. See, for example, PFG Foundation, *Genetics and Mainstream Medicine*.

pedigree transforms 'the family' into a complex assemblage of *families* and the genetics professional's moral commitment to care for 'the family' into something inherently ethically problematic. Chapter 3 goes on to illustrate the ethical problems created by the multiplicity of the family pedigree and the genetics professional's commitment to the family (described in Chapter 2) through an exploration of the difficulties arising for genetics professionals out of the differences and similarities between the family understood as biological connectedness on the one hand and as social relatedness on the other. Like those in Chapters 2 and 3, the cases discussed in Chapter 4 are also ones in which ethical problems are created around the commitments of genetics professionals by the everyday practices of clinical genetics. Taking reproductive decision-making as its focus, this chapter explores how the genetics professional's commitment to patient-centredness is turned into an ethical problem by the practices of information-giving, non-directiveness and value-neutrality. And Chapter 5 examines how the multi-professional context of clinical genetics can lead to the emergence of ethical problems as different professional groups adopt practices in which different emphases are placed on important moral commitments and their relative importance.

Reflecting upon the discussion in the previous four chapters, and the interest among genetics professionals in exploring the ethical dimensions of their practice – as exemplified by their attendance at the Genethics Club – Chapter 6 examines the implications of the genetics professional's commitment to the idea that good practice requires not only that attention be paid to the clinical or medical aspects of their day-to-day work with patients and families, but also to what might be thought of as the *moral craft* of genetics. Drawing upon the cases presented in previous chapters, this chapter begins with an investigation of some of the ways in which the complexities of practice and of family life mean that what are otherwise stable and unreflective moral practices and commitments – patient-centredness, care for the patient and the family – can be rendered provisional and unstable by the everyday practices of clinical genetics. Against this background of instability, it becomes clear that it is primarily the ongoing *moral work* of the genetics professional which sustains good practice. However, as the discussion of cases in earlier chapters shows, although the moral work of the genetics professional is often successful in holding the moral practices of day-to-day genetics together, there are many situations in which the commitments and value judgements which inform good practice, and in fact the moral work by which this is sustained, can themselves emerge as important ethical problems. These problems are significant for genetics professionals because they bring into question and render uncertain the very question of what is to count as good practice and as doing a job well. The chapter concludes by exploring the central role of what I call *moral craft* in this context, and the part played by the Genetics Club therein.

Chapter 7, the book's final chapter, adopts a slightly different approach to those preceding it. Drawing on the analysis in the book as a whole, that is, on the ways in which the moral commitments informing day-to-day practices in genetics emerge as ethically problematic for genetics professionals, Chapter 7 examines the Genethics Club as a form of empirical bioethics – a method for both doing and understanding ethics. Addressing itself primarily to scholarly debates in bioethics and social science about ethics and the empirical, the chapter explores the methodological implications of the discussion in previous chapters for empirical bioethics and for ways of understanding contemporary genetics and genomics practice.

As the discussion unfolds throughout this book, it will become apparent that the everyday practices of genetics professionals are guided by a number of relatively stable, shared moral commitments and that in the practice of day-to-day clinical genetics these moral commitments are problematised – turned into ethical problems – by the very practices of clinical genetics themselves.[16] But it also becomes apparent that it would be a mistake to think that these ethical problems are something that can or should be dispensed with or 'resolved' or that the existence of ethical problems in genetics means that there is a *problem with genetics*. On the contrary, I have come to believe through my observations and analysis that such problems – which emerge out of the engagement of genetics practice and the social world – are what much of genetics practice is about. One of the implications of this belief is that the provision of answers or solutions to the ethical problems in genetics practice is not a principal aim of this book.

---

[16] I discuss the relation between morals and ethics in Chapter 6.

2　The patient in the families

Arrivals

People attend consultations with genetics professionals for a variety of reasons and arrive by a number of different routes. In practice, these routes tend to fall into three main types – though, as will become apparent, these distinctions are far from neat. In this chapter and throughout this book I shall refer to these types of referrals as: *probands, family member referrals* and *de facto referrals*.

Probands

In some cases the person who is referred to clinical genetics is thought at the time of referral to be the first member of their family to have been identified as being at risk or affected. I shall refer to such patients as *probands*.[1] Probands are often referred to clinical genetics by another health professional because of a diagnosis of an inherited condition in themselves or their child. This initial diagnosis might have arisen in a number of ways. It may be the result of a clinical test, such as an ECG, following symptoms. There is a wide range of clinical tests and investigations with the potential to reveal inherited conditions. In other cases, the referral might have been made because a dysmorphology syndrome is suspected by, or apparent to, a health professional, e.g. Marfan Syndrome.[2] Alternatively, while the patient may not have experienced any symptoms or have any discernable signs, an inherited condition or risk may have been identified during routine investigations, antenatally, pre-conception or during pregnancy. For these reasons, many probands will be women. While many referrals to genetics will follow a

---

[1] For the purposes of this book I adopt the definition of 'proband' as 'the person who draws medical attention to a family' – as used, for example, by West Midlands Regional Clinical Genetics Service (see www.bwhct.nhs.uk/genetics-index/genetics-wmrcgs-glossary.htm accessed 18 February 2011).

[2] A. Shaw, 'Interpreting images: diagnostic skill in the genetics clinic' (2003) 9 *Journal of the Royal Anthropological Institute*, 1, 39–55.

clinical diagnosis or suspicion of one, there are others in which a patient is referred following a diagnostic *genetic* test carried out in another specialty, e.g. neurology. Finally, a patient may be referred to clinical genetics by their doctor not because of the results of a test or because they have certain symptoms, but because of their own concerns about a perceived family history of a condition and what this might mean for them. This can arise in situations where a patient has become aware through conversations with other family members about the existence of a 'condition' in their family or a 'risk', e.g. a high incidence of breast cancer, and where their concern that they might be at risk has prompted them to contact their GP. Such conversations and the resulting contact with health professionals might, for example, be stimulated by discussion in the media about the condition, or about the availability of a new test, and following a risk assessment by their GP this might lead to a referral to clinical genetics as a proband.

Family member referrals

People who are referred to genetics as probands sometimes turn out to be members of families already well known to the genetics service. There are other cases in which patients are referred, not because of a diagnosis in themselves or their child or because of a concern about being at high risk, but because information about risk generated by a diagnosis elsewhere in their family means that they have come to the attention of a health professional responsible for their care as being 'at risk'. Here, patients are referred as *family member referrals*. There are two broad ways in which this might happen. The first is where a proband has provided genetics professionals with information about their family which, when combined with information about the diagnosis and mode of inheritance in them, makes it clear that identifiable family members are also at risk and that an intervention is available, e.g. screening, or the provision of information about reproductive choice. In such cases, the proband will be informed about the importance of their relative obtaining a referral to genetic services from their GP.[3] Often, the proband will be given a letter or information leaflet to pass on to their relative. Sometimes, where there is a significant chance that the condition will arise in a relative and where there is an evidence-based intervention they could have, or where there is a concern that the proband may not pass the information on or may be estranged from relatives, the genetics unit may attempt to liaise with the

---

[3] L. D'Agincourt-Canning, 'Experiences of genetic risk: disclosure and the gendering of responsibility' (2001) 15 *Bioethics*, 3, 231–247.

GP of the at-risk family member directly. In rare cases and where the GP is not available to help, the at-risk relative may be contacted directly to be informed of the options available to them.

These approaches are possible where the consultation with a proband leads to awareness of risk in *identifiable* individuals related to them. In some cases, however, a more distributed and non-specific risk is identified, i.e. an awareness that this is an at-risk family.[4] In such situations a 'to whom it may concern' letter containing information about the condition is given to the proband, along with advice to pass this on to members of their wider family. The letter will include information about the condition and advice to recipients to contact their GP who will facilitate a referral to genetics. Inevitably, while these letters will in some cases permeate quite widely throughout a family, reaching family members with whom the proband has no personal contact and who may live in different parts of the country or in other countries, in others the distribution of the letter will be rather more limited or not occur at all.

De facto referrals

A third way in which a person can become a patient in clinical genetics is where they are brought along to a consultation by a relative, who may themselves be either a proband or a family member referral, and become patients even though they have not received an appointment letter. It is not unheard of, for example, for a patient who has received a referral to clinical genetics because of an assessment of their own risk to pre-empt the family member referral process and to bring one or more family members along to the consultation with them. In such cases, these family members become *de facto* patients.

Constructing pedigrees[5]

When patients first arrive in clinical genetics,[6] whether as probands, family member referrals or de facto referrals, they are seen by a counsellor and/or a geneticist who begins by clarifying who they were referred by, why they are there and what they are hoping to get out of their

---

[4] K. Featherstone, P. Atkinson, A. Bharadwaj and A. Clarke, *Risky Relations: Family, Kinship and the New Genetics* (Oxford: Berg, 2006).

[5] NHS National Genetics Education and Development Centre, *Taking and Drawing a Family History* (Birmingham: NHS National Genetics Education and Development Centre, 2008); Clinical Genetics Society, *Guidelines for Pedigree Drawing* (Birmingham: Clinical Genetics Society, 2001) available at www.clingensoc.org/Docs/Standards/CGSPedigree.pdf (accessed 29 July 2011).

[6] This initial meeting can in some cases take place at the patient's home.

consultation. Early on in this first consultation, the importance of health-related information about their family members will be explained. The counsellor and/or geneticist will ask the patient about details of their family history and structure, and after this a 'family pedigree' will be created. The family pedigree and its construction are fundamental to the practice of clinical genetics.[7] The pedigree, in combination with other tools, is used for the estimation of risk, the establishment of the mode of inheritance and the clarification of any implications for future management, treatment or screening for the patient, for pregnancies, and for other family members.[8] Following interpretation of the pedigree, decisions will be made about the patient's care, advice about risk and so on. Decisions will also be made about the most appropriate mechanism for informing members of the wider family about their risk.

In general the process of working up a family pedigree begins with the eliciting of information about the patient themselves. The patient is entered on the page (or the screen) as a symbol (a square or a circle; denoting male or female) along with their current age, their diagnosis (if any) and their age at the time of diagnosis. Following this, they are asked how many sisters or brothers they have, and these are also added to the diagram as circles or squares. When the structure of this first generation of the family is set out on the pedigree, each sibling is discussed in turn and the patient is asked for details about their medical history. This will include their current age, their date of birth, relevant medical history including diagnoses and age at diagnosis, date and cause of death if relevant, whether they were tested genetically and the results of genetic tests if these are known. They will also be asked whether the relatives are, or ever have been, in contact with another clinical genetics unit. All of this information is added to the pedigree. Once gathering information about this first generation is completed, the patient is asked for information about the children of each of the people previously recorded. Careful questions will also be asked about possible miscarriages, still-births and abortions, and about deaths in childhood. They will also be asked to make sure they have not forgotten anyone (people who live abroad, etc.). After this, the conversation moves to other generations, e.g. parents, aunts and uncles, grandparents and similar questions are asked until a

---

[7] Y. Nugaka and A. Cambrosio, 'Medical pedigrees and the visual production of family disease in Canadian and Japanese genetic counselling practice', in M.A. Elston (ed.) *The Sociology of Medical Science and Technology* (Oxford: Blackwell, 1997), pp. 29–56; P. Harper, *Practical Genetic Counselling*, sixth edition (London: Edward Arnold, 2004), p. 5.

[8] P. Rose, 'Taking a family history', in P. Rose and A. Lucassen, *Practical Genetics for Primary Care* (Oxford University Press, 1999), pp. 57–75; NHS National Genetics Education and Development Centre, *Taking and Drawing a Family History*.

three- or four-generation pedigree has been completed. When it is completed, a family pedigree looks something like this:

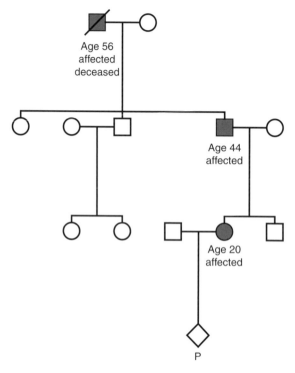

Figure 1

Verification of the pedigree

Information provided by a patient for the purposes of constructing the family pedigree inevitably has a range of sources. In some cases, this information will be based upon what the patient believes to be true – given conversations with other family members for example – and inevitably some of the details given about health or disease will be incorrect, inaccurate or unclear.[9] Such inaccuracies can be highly relevant to

---

[9] D. Armstrong, S. Michie and T. Marteau, 'Revealed identity: a study of the process of genetic counselling' (1998) 47 *Social Science and Medicine*, 11, 1653–1658; A. Lucassen, R. Wheeler and M. Parker, 'Implications of data protection legislation for family history' (2006) 332 *British Medical Journal*, 299–301; F. Kee, L. Tiret, J.Y. Robo, V. Nicaud, E. McCrum, A. Evans and F. Cambien, 'Reliability of reported family history of myocardial infarction' (1993) 307 *British Medical Journal*, 6918, 1528–1530.

practice and might include: people who are reported as having had a diagnosis of breast cancer when they in fact had no such diagnosis, e.g. it was a benign lump; people who are described as having had a cancer in one location when in fact it was in another, e.g. ovarian cancer when it was in fact intestinal; and people who have been described as having been completely healthy when in fact they were affected by an inherited condition. Many such kinds of inaccuracy are possible, with significance for diagnosis, advice and treatment, and for this reason it is considered to be important, as far as possible, for the clinical geneticist or counsellor to verify the family pedigree using information from other sources. These might include: the relative's GP, the hospital at which they were treated, disease registries, public records or other documentation, e.g. death certificates located by the patient.

As part of the process of verification, consent is obtained wherever possible from relatives for permission to access their records, or to contact their GP or other doctors.[10] Inevitably, some of these relatives are no longer alive or are not contactable. In such cases, particularly in the case of first- or second-degree relatives, the patient – i.e. the person currently being seen – tends to be asked to give consent (verbal or written) to release this information. In the case of more distant relatives, e.g. grandparents, where these relatives have a living spouse or adult child, some clinics, but not all, ask the patient to approach these relatives for permission. In practice, however, it is unlikely that confirmation of a diagnosis in one estranged or very distant relative will be critical to a risk assessment.

In all cases where information in the pedigree is confirmed, or where additional information becomes available through the process of verification, this fact, i.e. the source of the information, is recorded in the family notes.

Ethics and practices

This is a book about the ways in which everyday practices in clinical genetics such as those described above can come to be seen as ethically problematic. It will become increasingly apparent in subsequent chapters that this can occur in a number of multifaceted and interdependent ways. I begin in this first chapter with an exploration of the ways in which the conception of the 'patient in the family' and of the genetics professional as 'family practitioner', in combination with the material

[10] Joint Committee on Medical Genetics, *Consent and Confidentiality in Genetic Practice: Guidance on Genetic Testing and Sharing Genetic Information* (London: Royal College of Physicians of London, 2006), p. 12.

and other practices described above, e.g. the creation and recording of the family pedigree, can lead to the emergence of day-to-day practice in clinical genetics as an ethical problem.

(i)   The burdens of knowledge

The fact that clinical genetics units tend to work with families in the ways outlined above, often over many years, and work with rare and serious conditions, means that genetics professionals sometimes come to know several generations and 'branches' of at-risk families very well. Genetics services are regionally distributed, tending to cover quite large populations, and this means that different branches of such families will often be seen by genetics professionals in the same clinic and in many cases, given the tendency to specialise, by the very same health professional. It is also not uncommon for some families to be well known across different regional services and thereby to the genetics 'community' more widely.

Clinical genetics became well established as a medical speciality both in the United States and in Europe in the 1960s.[11] This long history of practice means that many of the families currently being seen by clinical genetics services have been in a relationship with these services from well before the advent of most genetic testing.[12] The following account is not an uncommon situation in this respect:

We've got a large family in our service, all of whom still live within the region, or most of them do, who carry BRCA1 and were first reported in … about 1968 and obviously when the gene became identified they were tested … and [some of them were] found to be positive. And now there are lots of different strands of the family, and one young woman came to see me because she knew her grandmother was a carrier … and she also knew that her mother who lives in [another country] [was] a patient of mine.

This focus on the family and on the care of the family can lead to enduring, even if intermittent, relationships between genetics professionals and family members. However, while offering important benefits, this orientation towards the family can sometimes lead to situations in which the recording or remembering of familial information produces problems as well as solutions. One way this can happen is in situations where, because of the genetics professional's long-standing relationship

[11] P. Harper, *A Short History of Medical Genetics* (Oxford University Press, 2008), pp. 271–312.
[12] Although the majority of genetic tests only became available from the 1990s onwards, a small number of tests were available before this.

with other family members, she knows more about the family than the patient in front of her does. An example of this is where a person referred as a *proband* is recognised as coming from a 'known family'.

[One of the main ethical issues arising] is ... the [situation] where you have information about someone based on other family members that they don't know about. How do you convey that information without breaching confidentiality? Prime example being a [inherited condition] family, for instance, where I knew a lot about the natural history of their particular gene having seen twenty or so of their relatives but they didn't know anything about the rest of the family which made it difficult to give them [advice]. Well, I could give them information quite easily because I knew quite a lot about what the outcome was likely to be but that might have appeared to be [offering] a rather false sense of security [because] they didn't know [that I knew] about the rest of the family. So if they do a lot of reading, which of course a lot of patients do, they'll say 'well how on earth can you say all these things with such certainty?'

For the genetics professional this situation is ethically problematic for a number of reasons. They are in a situation in which they have information that could be of help to their patient but which is only credible when understood in the context of other information about the wider family. The genetics professional's reassurance makes no sense without this supplementary information. Should any of this be disclosed? What should happen if the patient asks for reasons why they are not, in fact, at risk? Situations in which a patient thinks that they are at risk but are known not to be, because of the clinician's knowledge of the family, are not uncommon and here the everyday practice of working with families becomes ethically problematic because it is in tension with another feature of good practice, namely 'confidentiality'. In the case described above the relevant information concerns the absence of risk. In others it will be about the existence of unsuspected risk. In either situation genetics professionals can feel torn between the need to provide the best possible care to their patient on the one hand and their duty of confidentiality to other family members on the other.

(ii)   The master pedigree and the family file

In the case described above, problematic knowledge is produced by the familial nature of genetic practice and the familial experience of the genetics professional. Knowledge practices relating to the family in clinical genetics can also be made ethically problematic by the movement and juxtaposition of patient records.

Following their initial consultation, a patient's notes are stored in a file – either paper or electronic – containing information relating to their care, such as correspondence, test results and family pedigrees. Because of the perceived importance of relationships between different family members for clinical genetics and because health professionals in genetics tend to think of themselves as 'family practitioners', the notes of the individual patients within a family are stored in ways that allow them, and the information in them, to be linked. The most common way in which this is achieved is through the creation of what is sometimes called the 'family file' – a folder or a database bringing together all of the notes of the individual members of the same family in a single location for convenience.[13] Although the records are brought together in a family file, each individual set of notes will tend to contain a family pedigree based on information provided by that individual, and modified in the light of verification. Inevitably – given the possibility that different family members will have different understandings of the health of their relatives – the information in each of these pedigrees about the family, and indeed about the same individuals, will sometimes be very different. For this reason, it is standard practice to create a 'master pedigree' of the family, based on the information available in all the individual records, which is a best guess at the 'correct' family pedigree – in order to ensure appropriate care and counselling. In some settings, and in some conditions, individual notes are not stored together in a family file but are stored separately in individual patient files and given 'codes' which enable these individual files to be brought together if necessary.[14] This is also, however, in effect to construct a virtual family file, with the potential to be brought into existence when necessary. In either case the construction and juxtaposition of multiple individual family pedigrees and the 'master pedigree' in the family file – whether virtual or actual – means that a familial resource has been created in which 'the family' is constituted as an assemblage of many different potentially conflicting 'families'.

The bringing together of the records of individual patients into a single resource, the 'family file', and the translocation of information from individual pedigrees to the master pedigree, is intended to facilitate understanding of the family as a 'whole' and is seen by genetics professionals as an important tool for clinical practice and counselling.

---

[13] The precise ways in which records are stored vary between genetics services and also to some extent between different conditions but, in general, there is something like this kind of juxtaposition of the notes and pedigrees constructed with different individual family members, and something along the lines of a 'master pedigree' which represents the genetics professionals' best guess at the correct family history.

[14] Huntington's Disease family records are sometimes organised in this kind of way, for example.

In combination with the genetics professional's knowledge and experience, however, it also has the potential to lead to ethical problems. This is because the bringing together and 'verification' of individual pedigrees in the creation of the master pedigree and of the family file can generate the production of an assemblage of 'families' which is inherently conflictual and which no individual family member would be likely to recognise, and which may, moreover – as will become apparent in subsequent chapters – include information of which no one in the family is aware. That this is at least in part a process brought about by the translocation of material objects and/or electronic data is illustrated by situations where a patient moves from one clinic to another and the insertion of their file into an existing family file leads to a radical transformation of the master pedigree. The patient and 'the family' thus emerge as an ethical problem anew.

We saw a woman who was concerned about her family history of cancer ... She had a family history, but it wasn't very significant and we were reassuring about it ... She [also] said that she was concerned about her two daughters ... as she knew that there was also a family history on their father's side. His sister had had ovarian cancer and there was further family history [but] she didn't know the details. They had quite an unusual surname and so my colleague said, I'll check his name against a database we hold of known mutation carriers and see if ... I went back to this woman saying ... I've checked our records and can see no connections with the families we know of with genetic predisposition ... But then we subsequently found out through one of the trainee counsellors who drew together another pedigree that actually he was quite distantly related to a known BRCA1 carrier and that this BRCA1 carrier had actually given consent for the result to be disseminated but it [had not] got down to this branch of the family yet. This meant that there wasn't an issue about disclosure to [the father] because eventually it would have been disseminated to him in any case ... but the issue that arose for us [concerned] what we were able to tell the woman [who consulted us] because she was separated from him and [it had no direct relevance] to her – she was asking on behalf of her daughters but her daughters were adults and therefore it wasn't clear to us whether we should tell their mother or should we say we've got some more information but it's only of relevance to the daughters? ... in the end we just got terribly confused about what we could say to who and she was the only patient that we had seen. Nobody else had come forward to us.

Taken together, the cases discussed above describe situations in which working with families and storing patient records in certain kinds of ways can produce knowledge with the potential to transform such practices into ethical problems. The ethical problem in the cases described above takes the form of a question about whether such knowledge, with its origins in experience of consultations with other family members or as an artefact of bringing individual records together in a family file, should be available for the treatment and counselling of family members. Or, whether such information should be seen as personal and as confidential to those from whom it was obtained, even if this results in care that is less than optimal in clinical terms. If the latter, the question arises as to whether this information should be stored in a family file or incorporated into a master pedigree at all, without the consent of those whose individual records contribute to it.

(iii)   Problematic interdependence

In the cases described in the sections above, the ethical challenge to family-oriented practice arises because of information already held by the genetics professional by virtue of their work with the patient's family or because of the way that family records are stored. To some extent the problem in such cases is a result of the fact that the information is to hand – the genetics professional *remembers* another case in the same family or *comes across* something relevant by opening a file or during the construction of the master pedigree. There are other cases, however, where the genetics professional does not have the information to hand but knows that it could be made available by seeking out the test results of a family member, by accessing and testing a blood sample, or by reading the (easily accessible) file of another patient in the family. Knowledge of this less proximate kind generates two quite different ethical questions for genetics professionals. First, is there a morally significant difference between situations in which the genetics professional simply has information relevant to a patient's care to hand and those in which she would have to actively seek it out? Second, is there a morally significant difference between information stored in a file, e.g. about an adoption, and that arising out of tests on accessible samples?

There are a number of ways in which the clinical care of one family member can be dependent upon information derived from others which have the potential to make these ethical problems feel very real for genetics professionals. I have already described the construction of the family pedigree and its role in assessing risk and mode of inheritance. This is an example of a way in which a patient's care (and access to care through a risk assessment) can depend upon the active seeking out of information about other family members – by asking the proband, through the verification of the pedigree, or through the fairly routine practice of searching databases to see whether the patient comes from a 'known family'. A key additional way in which family members are dependent upon others for their care and treatment arises out of a particular combination of the limitations of certain types of genetic tests and the nature of many disease-causing mutations.[15] There are two main ways in which this manifests itself. First, in some cases the disease-causing mutation is either unique to the family or is very rare (perhaps one on which little research has been carried out), and this means that a test for the mutation is only available to members of the wider family if the mutation has been identified in at least one affected family member and the details of the mutation are accessible. That is, if it is known what to test for. Second, and relatedly, there are some relatively common conditions which can be caused by any one of a very large number of different mutations, some of which are well known and for which a test is available, and some of which are rare forms for which no genetic test is widely available. Examples might be breast cancer, familial adenomatous polyposis, cystic fibrosis and Duchenne muscular dystrophy. In such conditions the fact that there might be a standard widely available test which tests for the majority of well-known mutations but not for the rarer variants means that a negative test result (i.e. a 'good news' result) using the widely available test does not always, when interpreted in the light of a particular family history, reduce the patient's risk significantly because it is possible that they have one of the rarer variants. In such cases, a negative test result may be insufficient to take a patient out of the high-risk group and therefore does not alter their clinical management. Here the only way to provide a test with the potential to be of real benefit to a patient is by testing for a specific disease-causing mutation identified in a relative known to have been affected with the condition.

It will be apparent that in both cases this combination of factors creates a situation in which a genetics professional is unable to provide a useful test to a patient except in combination with information from other family members. In other words, optimal care for the patient is only possible to the extent to which the patient can be located within a particular family topology.[16] Cases like this can lead to scenarios in which the possibility of testing and counselling a patient is dependent upon the active seeking out of familial information. For while it may sometimes be the case that the genetics professional caring for the patient remembers the name of the mutation because of her knowledge of other family members, it is more likely that, although she will not have it to hand, she will know where to find it, or whom to ask. The problem created here is once again whether, and if so in what

---

[15] Joint Committee on Medical Genetics, *Consent and Confidentiality in Genetic Practice*, p. 11.
[16] This is discussed further in Chapter 3.

circumstances, genetics professionals should use familial information in the treatment and care of individual family members. If it is accepted that it is good practice for genetics professionals to use their (to hand) experience and knowledge of a family to provide the best possible care to their patients does this also mean that it is ethical for them to *seek out* familial information and use it to the same ends, e.g. to look in the files of known family members for the names of familial mutations which will make testing possible?

In many instances, the most straightforward way of answering the question as to whether or not such information should be used will be to contact the source of the information directly, i.e. the other family member, and ask for their permission.[17] However, while in many cases this will provide a solution, there are others in which the consent process itself generates new ethical problems – often because the relative has not given consent.

A pregnant woman wanted her fetus tested for cystic fibrosis because of a history of the condition in her family. When we carried out the test, the result (for standard common mutations) was negative but the concern was that the family mutation might be a rare one and the standard test might have missed it because the standard kit is known to miss 15 per cent of known mutations. Someone else in the family has had carrier testing for cystic fibrosis and so the lab does hold the details, but they are refusing to release details of the mutation. Apparently the woman who had the original test didn't want family members to terminate pregnancies. The question is, should the lab do the test (using the other family member's result) but without telling the person from whom this information was obtained?

When approached for mutational information which would make a test available for a family member of one of their patients, different genetics professionals and different medical specialties can have divergent views about releasing this information and about the need for consent from the person who was the original source of it.[18] In the case above, for example, laboratory staff refuse to release the information because of concerns about a breach of confidentiality and the need to obtain consent. But making access to testing and reproductive information dependent upon the wishes of relatives and subject to their veto is itself not ethically unproblematic. Should a woman's access to prenatal testing be dependent upon her relatives' views about abortion?

[17] N. Hallowell, 'Doing the right thing: genetic risk and responsibility' (1999) 21 *Sociology of Health and Illness*, 5, 597–621.
[18] The implications of multi-professional practice for the ethics of clinical genetics are explored in Chapter 5.

There are some situations in which the very process of seeking consent is itself seen as ethically problematic by health professionals. In the following case, for example, the concern is not that the relatives might refuse consent but that the process of seeking consent might have an impact on the family.

The clinic was approached by the aunt and uncle of a proband. They wanted to have carrier testing for cystic fibrosis because they knew that their nephew, the clinic's patient, had been diagnosed with cystic fibrosis. They said that they came to the clinic directly because they didn't want to go to the parents of the child, the aunt's sister, to talk about this because they didn't want her to know that they are going for testing and because they were worried about the risk in the family. The mutation details of the nephew are known by the clinic and the test could easily be carried out, but is it acceptable to use these details to carry out the test? The couple say that it isn't possible for them to talk to their nephew's mother about this.

On occasion, it is not access to mutational information but rather access to and testing of a sample that is required. This may be because, while the sample was collected during the treatment of a family member, a test has not yet been carried out on it, or a different test is now indicated. One example of this is where there is a need to use an affected family member as a 'positive control' to verify a test in a patient, or where such testing is required for quality assurance in the use of a test for a mutation unique to a particular family. To what extent should consent be required in such circumstances?

A male patient was affected with familial adenomatous polyposis (FAP) before testing became available. He had his colon removed. Later on the mutation in the family became known. Some time after this, the patient's daughter arrived at the clinic for a predictive test. Blood was taken from her. For the test to be most accurate, however, DNA was needed from another affected person in the family as a positive control (to control for private polymorphisms at primer binding site). The problem is that the clinician – who is in another centre – refused to disclose details of family mutation without consent from someone who had been tested. Should consent be necessary for testing in this way? I agree that it would probably be necessary if the sample was being used to test the relative, but is it really necessary for quality assurance (QA) for polymorphisms in the same family?

There are a number of other contexts in which the obtaining, or even the seeking, of consent can be problematic. These include, for example, situations in which a relative from whom information or a sample is required is terminally ill, or where a potential – perhaps the only – source of genetic information is a patient or a family member who does not have the capacity to provide valid consent.

The problems genetics professionals face in the situations described in this section are to do with having, or having relatively easy access to, knowledge about the patient's family with the potential to be of real benefit to their patient but being unsure about whether it is right to use such information, or to actively seek it out (either by looking in a record, by contacting a colleague or by testing an existing sample from another family member), without the consent of relatives. In some cases this involves no more than looking in a file for mutational information and such information has the potential to be of benefit in a number of important ways: the potential to alleviate anxiety; the potential to ensure that a patient has appropriate surveillance, information and treatment; access to prenatal testing and reproductive information; information that will enable them to avoid serious but in their case pointless, prophylactic surgery, etc.[19] To what extent are mutational details 'personal' information and to what extent should the availability of such information for the treatment and counselling of patients be dependent upon the consent of their relatives, or subject to the problems associated with the obtaining of consent described above? Should genetics professionals be allowed to use all of the information available to them to provide the best care they can to their patients, even if this involves actively seeking out such information?[20]

(iv)   Obligations to inform 'the family'

Previous sections have highlighted the potential for information derived from the wider family to be of value to patients. The situations described thus far have concerned genetics professionals who have, or have relatively easy access to, information that may be of use to the person sitting in front of them. Situations also arise in which the genetics professional has information from her own patient which may be of value to other family members (who may or may not be patients of the same clinician, or even patients at all) and feels an obligation to make efforts to ensure that this information is shared with them or with the health professionals responsible for their care. Such information has the potential to be of value to family members in the same ways that, as described above, information from other family members may be of benefit to the genetics professional's own patients. But if they don't know about the risk,

---

[19] R.E. Ashcroft, A. Lucassen, M. Parker, G. Widdershoven and M. Verkerk (eds.) *Case Analysis in Clinical Ethics* (Cambridge University Press, 2005).

[20] Joint Committee on Medical Genetics, *Consent and Confidentiality in Genetic Practice*, p. 11.

they cannot seek help. The sense of obligation is strengthened in these cases by the fact that genetics professionals see themselves as family practitioners treating and supporting families rather than individuals, and by the fact that this familial distribution of obligation is enshrined in their professional guidelines. It is also reinforced by the creation of the family file and of the master pedigree which is in a sense a material enactment of an emergent pattern of obligations both for the patient and for the genetics professional.

Standard practice in situations where family members (or the family more generically) are identified as being 'at risk' was described in the section on 'family referrals' above. In situations where information arising in the care of a patient is of relevance to other identifiable family members, the patient is informed about the importance of sharing such information and is advised to encourage these relatives to contact their GP. In situations where there is a general risk in the family but particular individuals have not been identified, a contact letter with basic information is given to the proband to share with their relatives. While in some families information of this kind will be distributed effectively and appropriately there will inevitably be families where this is not the case for a range of different reasons (many of which will be discussed in the next chapter).[21] In some cases, the less–than–complete dissemination of knowledge in the family comes to the attention of genetics professionals and this knowledge too can be productive of ethical problems.[22]

Because of her awareness of a family history, a young woman came for testing for a condition with the potential to cause thyroid cancer. She tested negative but we were concerned in our conversations with her that the information about the risk had not been spread more widely in the family. We had spoken to her father in the past and had assumed that because of what he said at the time that he would have passed it on to the wider family. But our conversations with his daughter raised some doubts that this hadn't in fact happened. At about the same time an aunt appeared and was diagnosed with thyroid cancer. This could have been avoided by an earlier prophylactic thyroidectomy but she hadn't been told that [she was at risk] and that a genetic test was available. At the time we were treating the father we did know that this branch of the family existed and could possibly with some effort have found their contact details. But, following standard practice we went through him. In this case we don't think that there was any malicious or wilful non-disclosure on the part of the father – he just hadn't got round to it. This raises questions for us about

[21] A. Clarke, M. Richards, L. Kerzin-Storrar, et al., 'Genetic professionals' reports of nondisclosure of genetic risk information within families' (2005) 13 European Journal of Human Genetics, 556–562; Featherstone et al., Risky Relations, pp. 91–116.

[22] Clarke et al., 'Genetic professionals' reports of nondisclosure'.

our practice. Should we have contacted [the at-risk relatives we knew about] directly?

In some cases such difficulties can be generated by the absence of any suitable familial route for the dissemination of information.

One of our patients is a mother with mild learning difficulties. She already has two sons with Fragile X. The family is known to social services and she was referred to us for genetic counselling. The genetics team knows that there is a nephew living nearby who has similar problems. We believe that it is possible that the nephew also has Fragile X but has never been diagnosed. We are not sure whether the family is aware and we feel a duty to ensure that this other branch of the family is offered genetic counselling and testing too. What should we do? I have been trying to go through the mother but have had no response as yet. Should I wait for her sister to contact genetics? Should I ask social services to carry a message? I have also tried to conduct my own enquiries through contacts with other clinical and lab colleagues but they have told me that this is confidential.

One set of practical ethical questions with which genetics professionals are faced in such cases concerns what constitutes a reasonable effort to contact relatives. When, if ever, is it sufficient to have provided information to the patient and to have advised them of the importance of passing this information on to their relatives? Is there an obligation in some or all cases to follow up and to check that information has in fact been disseminated? What are a genetics professional's obligations when she has good reason to believe that this information is not being communicated or is being communicated inaccurately? Do genetics professionals have an obligation to help patients to share information about risks and the availability of interventions with relatives? If so, what are the limits of these obligations? Current practice, as was described above, is to contact relatives via their GPs or the patient. More recently, however, some have begun to ask whether it might in fact be better to contact relatives directly.[23] While this could itself be problematic – because it would involve contacting people out of the blue – there may be cases, as below, where there appears to be no other means of communication.

Clinical geneticists had been working with a patient for several years who recently died aged thirty-eight, of FAP. Although he was divorced at the time of his death the geneticists know that he had an eight-year-old daughter and feel that they have a duty to ensure that she and her mother know about the diagnosis, risk and availability of screening. The team are not sure that this

---

[23] A.J. Newson and S.E. Humphries, 'Cascade testing in familial hypercholesterolaemia: how should family members be contacted?' (2005) 13 *European Journal of Human Genetics*, 401–408.

information has been shared. Daughter is at 50 per cent risk and screening can start at fourteen. The mother and daughter's names are known and the team knows where they live and their GP's name.

There are some situations in which the question of the limits of the obligations of health professionals to inform families concerns the allocation of resources, including clinician and administrative time. Say there is a situation, for example, where a new test with relevance to patients previously seen becomes available. Do clinical genetics units have an obligation to go through all their records and contact the members of families with the potential to benefit from the new test? Does knowledge of families and the enduring existence of the family file create a duty to keep them up to date with developments in technology?

We have had letters from one centre, for example, telling us that they can now find carriers for spinal muscular atrophy (SMA). This is a significant advance. In this case we have written to all of the SMA families on our list. But what are our duties in this respect, i.e. keeping people up to date with developments?

In the cases discussed above, the genetics professionals' conception of themselves as family practitioners, that is, as having obligations to 'the family', is rendered deeply problematic by their recognition in particular contexts of the many conflicting practical and ethical implications of taking on a responsibility to care for a wide range of family members. Such cases present difficult questions about both the nature and scope of these familial obligations: for, if genetics professionals do have obligations to the family, when in any case might it be reasonable to say that such obligations have been met? The account developed above of the practices involved in the construction and verification of the family pedigree and its incorporation into the master pedigree and the family file, through which 'the family' is constituted as an assemblage of many different 'families', suggests a profoundly unsettling answer to this question. For it implies that the genetics professional's obligation to 'the' or to 'a' family is always potentially conflictual and is one that can frequently never be fully met.

(v)   *Situations in which a patient refuses permission to share information*

While clinicians working in genetics see themselves as having a duty of care to families and for the dissemination of relevant familial information, they also see themselves as having important obligations to their patient. In most cases, these two duties pull in the same direction and it is possible both to care for the patient and also through them to ensure (to some extent at least) that information and hence screening and treatment are made available to the at-risk members of their family. There are, however, as has already been seen, situations in which these duties pull in different directions. These are situations in which the care of the individual patient can be both dependent upon familial practice (i.e. through its dependence on family pedigrees, etc. as set out in sections i–iii above) and at the same time in tension with familial practice.[24] Perhaps the quintessential example of this is where a patient in full knowledge of their potential benefits to others refuses to share information with members of their family.[25] Such cases are not very common but they loom large.

A woman in our clinic whose mother is affected by myotonic dystrophy wants a predictive genetic test. She says that her mother does not know that she has come to the clinic. Her brother doesn't know about his mother's diagnosis. Her pregnant cousin also doesn't know. Initial discussions with our patient have focused on the implications of this test and of the information about the diagnosis for other family members. As part of this process she was given some information to give to her family members but she says that she doesn't want to do this.

When such cases occur, genetics professionals place a lot of emphasis on supporting the patient and encouraging communication in the family. They will often take the view that this takes time and are very skilled at getting families to talk. Nevertheless, cases do arise in which, despite the best efforts of the genetics professional, patients are clear that they do not want information to be shared with their relatives and will find ways of avoiding dissemination. In other cases, allowing time for a patient to come around to the view that they should share the information with their relatives will itself put other family members at risk. In the following example, the usefulness of the information is time-limited by the realities of pregnancy.

Helen Cross's four-year-old son has just had Duchenne muscular dystrophy (DMD) diagnosed. Genetic testing confirms the diagnosis and shows that she is a carrier for the mutation. Mrs Cross's sister, Penelope Yates, is ten weeks pregnant. Mrs Yates's obstetrician referred her to the genetics team after she told him that her nephew had speech and development delay. She told him that although she was not close to her sister and had not discussed it with her, she was concerned about the implications for her own pregnancy. In her

---

[24] General Medical Council, *Confidentiality* (London: General Medical Council, 2009).

[25] C. Novas and N. Rose, 'Genetic risk and the birth of the somatic individual' (2000) 29 *Economy and Society*, 4, 485–513.

discussions with the clinical geneticist (who did not know at this stage that both sisters were patients in the same clinic), Mrs Yates made it clear that she would consider terminating a pregnancy if she knew that the fetus was affected with a serious inherited condition.

Speech and development delay are features of several conditions and would not of themselves indicate carrier-testing for DMD. In addition, because the Duchenne gene is large and several possible mutations exist, testing without information about which mutation is responsible for the nephew's condition is unlikely to be informative.

At her next meeting with her clinical geneticist, Mrs Cross says that she knows that her sister is pregnant and that she understands that her sister's baby could be affected. She says that she has not discussed this with her sister, partly because they don't really get on but also because she suspects that if her sister were to find out, and if the fetus turned out to be affected, she would terminate the pregnancy. Mrs Cross feels strongly that this would be wrong. She knows that her sister does not share her views, but Mrs Cross says she has thought long and hard about the issues and has decided that she wants her test results and information about her son to remain confidential.

All best efforts have been made to encourage the sisters to talk to each other and to share the information and that despite this Mrs Cross continues to refuse permission for this information to be shared with her sister.[26]

Sometimes, it is not that patients wish to withhold information from their family but that they wish to define just *who* is to count as a member of the family and who is not, and this may not map neatly onto those people the clinician considers to be most in need of the information.

A man aged thirty-five was diagnosed with stomach cancer. Two of his siblings had died of it and his mother died of uncontrolled diabetes. He gave blood and consent to share information 'with family'. A test on the sample confirmed the diagnosis. The sister and aunt were told and were very upset. But, after his death, his sister and aunt contacted the unit and insisted that they did not want information about the condition and risk to be shared with his wife. They said, it had no health implications for her, she would gossip and she 'loved a crisis'. They said that they were also concerned about 'marriageability' of the man's youngest brother. But who is a family member? What is the familial status of the wife?

These examples, in which patients refuse to share mutational and other information with relatives, provide another set of important test cases for genetics professionals of the familial dimensions of their practice. To what extent should such information be treated as a familial resource? To what extent should it be seen as personal information and its use subject to individual consent and the veto of relatives?[27]

---

[26] This case is also discussed in M. Parker and A. Lucassen, 'Genetic information: a joint account?' (2004) 329 *British Medical Journal*, 165–167.

[27] *Ibid.*; Clarke *et al.*, 'Genetic professionals' reports of nondisclosure'; Joint Committee on Medical Genetics, *Consent and Confidentiality in Genetic Practice*, p. 14.

Competing commitments to the patient and the families

The cases discussed in this chapter were presented as ethically problematic by genetics professionals who attended the Genethics Club. This suggests that clinical genetics practice is permeated by two incompatible and competing conceptualisations of the moral features of the clinical role, each of which is built into and to some extent created by the practices and material objects through which genetics practice is constituted.

Their professional guidelines emphasise that doctors should make the care of the patient their first concern.[28] In clinical genetics, the best care of the patient requires the collection and use of familial information. Examples include: the drawing-up of a family pedigree for risk assessment and for understanding modes of inheritance; the verification of the information in such pedigrees using medical records of family members; and the use of mutational information from other affected family members to make predictive testing available. The role of this information in the provision of optimal, or even *any*, care is apparent in the cases discussed in this chapter. For these reasons, genetics professionals place great value on the familial dimensions of their practice. What is a resource for the care of one family member also has the potential to be a resource for the care of other family members. The tendency to think in terms of 'families' rather than 'patients', combined with the use of family pedigrees, family files and the master pedigree, draws upon a conception of clinical genetics as a familial practice and of genetic information as a familial resource.

Like health professionals elsewhere in medicine, however, those in clinical genetics also see good practice and the care of the patient as requiring high standards of confidentiality and the obtaining of appropriate consent, and this is exemplified in the cases described above where genetics professionals express concern about using or sharing patient information without such consent.[29] These more patient-centred approaches to what it means to make the care of the patient one's first concern arise out of a quite different conceptualisation of clinical genetics practice and of the moral status of genetic information. This is one in which such information is understood to be personal and where,

[28] General Medical Council, *Good Medical Practice* (London: General Medical Council, 2006).

[29] Human Genetics Commission, *Inside Information: Balancing Interests in the Use of Personal Data* (London: UK Department of Health, 2002), pp. 63–64.

despite its potential as a familial resource, its use in the care of family members should be subject to the same rules of confidentiality and consent as applied elsewhere in medicine. By contrast with that outlined above, this approach implies that while familial information provided by the patient herself may appropriately be used for her care (setting aside for the moment the question of whether the consent of others to disclosure of this information has been obtained by the patient)[30] and the care of others if she gives consent, there should be no verification of this information without the explicit consent of those whose records are to be accessed, no use of information or experience gained in previous consultations with family members, no creation of a family file without the explicit consent of all those whose information is to be included, no creation of a 'master pedigree' and no use of familial mutational information in the testing of family members except with the consent of the original affected person or in very exceptional circumstances, i.e. those presenting a 'risk of death or serious harm'.[31]

This chapter has explored some of the ways in which the genetics professional's commitment to caring both for the patient and the family can become ethically problematic and in which conflict between and within these commitments is unavoidable. What the discussion of these cases has shown is that the genetics professional's commitment to both the patient and the family is rendered problematic, at least in part, because of a number of features of day-to-day practice in clinical genetics. Of particular significance in this regard are the construction and verification of the family pedigree, the establishment of the family file and – through various processes of 'verification' – the creation and maintenance of the master pedigree, as a consequence of which 'the family' emerges as an assemblage of 'families' and through which the relationship between the patient and 'the family' is transformed into one between the patient and 'the families'. This latter relationship, while not always – or even very often – conflictual in practice, is nevertheless, by definition, *disposed towards*, conflict and, as such, might be understood to be inherently likely to generate ethical problems.

In other words, the implication of the constitution of the family as an assemblage is that the family file and the master pedigree are to be imagined not as the kind of two-dimensional object exemplified by the diagram on page 18 but, rather, as an object in which change, uncertainty, duplication and multiplicity are both inherent and of profound moral significance. In the next chapter, I illustrate some of

---

[30] *Ibid.*, p. 69.
[31] General Medical Council, *Confidentiality*.

the implications of this reconceptualisation of the family as multiple through an exploration of the ethical problems which arise for genetics professionals out of the differences and similarities between the family understood as biological connectedness on the one hand and as social relatedness on the other. In so doing, I revisit some of the cases discussed above to highlight the ways in which different facets of the same pedigree come into life and have moral significance at different points and from different perspectives.

3   Elective affinities

[D]omains such as 'culture' and 'nature' appear to be linked by virtue of being at once similar and dissimilar. What makes the similarities is the effort to 'see' connections, what makes the dissimilarities is the 'recognition' of difference. Difference thereby becomes apparent from the simple fact of life: it is a connection from another angle. That is, what looks as though it is connected to one fact can also be connected to another.[1]

Two families in the pedigree

My aim in this chapter is to illustrate the multiplicity of the family pedigree and of the genetics professional's moral commitment to the family through an exploration of the implications of the family understood as both biology and culture.[2] In their practice, genetics professionals see themselves as committed to caring for the family in two important and related senses. The first of these is a commitment to the family understood in terms of patterns of biological connectedness and reproductive partnership. That is, to the family understood as *biology*.[3] Whether as *probands*, *family* referrals or *de facto* referrals, people come into contact with genetics services because of the possibility that they, or their biological relatives, are at risk of a genetic disorder. In relation to the family understood in this way, genetics professionals are primarily concerned with elucidating the implications of genetic relatedness and with ensuring, insofar as this is possible, that those who are at risk of an inherited disorder, either in themselves or their offspring, are informed,

---

J.W. Von Goethe, *Elective Affinities* (London: Penguin Books, 1971 [1809]).

[1] M. Strathern, *After Nature: English Kinship in the Late Twentieth Century* (Cambridge University Press, 1992), pp. 72–73. Emphasis removed from original.
[2] I return to the genetics professional's commitment to the individual patient – the other side of the tension described in Chapter 2 – in the following chapter.
[3] K. Featherstone, P. Atkinson, A. Bharadwaj and A. Clarke, *Risky Relations: Family, Kinship and the New Genetics* (Oxford: Berg, 2006), p. vii.

supported and, where appropriate, offered interventions such as testing and screening. This commitment to caring for the family understood as biology arises out of the genetics professional's clinical responsibility for the identification, prevention and treatment of inherited disorders and is the main reason for the existence of genetic services. While the primary role of the clinical genetics service is to ensure that members of at-risk families have access to counselling, diagnosis, risk assessment, predictive testing and screening, the execution of such tasks is nevertheless achieved in the context of engagement with family members as people. That is, through counselling, the encouragement of the dissemination of information, 'providing support to families at times of distress' and 'facilitat[ing] their decision-making processes'. What this means is that in their engagement with patients and families, genetics professionals encounter the family not only as biology but also at the same time as *culture*.[4] While these 'two families' do not map neatly onto one another, neither are they completely separable. In most cases there is a great deal of interplay between these forms of relatedness and the genetics professional's role involves working with people who are related to one another in a variety of different ways, both biological and social.

Enriched senses of biological relatedness

Prior to being identified as being 'at risk' of an inherited disorder, people may not think very much about the complexities of their biological relatedness to other members of their family.[5] Coming into contact with genetics services can dramatically change this, however, and inevitably has the effect of foregrounding relationality.[6] The previous chapter showed how the material and other practices of clinical genetics both illuminate and produce relationality. That is what they are there for. On arrival in clinical genetics, whether as probands, family referrals or de facto referrals, patients are invited, through the construction of the family pedigree, to map out their biological relatedness to others across three or four generations and multiple branches of the family and this is then transcribed by the genetics professional.

---

[4] It is worth noting here that the genetics professionals who attend the Genethics Club work with a wide range of families and tend to have practical experience of diversity and realities of relationships as lived in the United Kingdom today. It is important not to assume, therefore, that the concept of 'the family' being used in these cases is that of the 'nuclear' or 'extended' family in an unproblematic sense.

[5] Featherstone *et al.*, *Risky Relations*, p. 28.

[6] *Ibid.*, p.74.

'Behind the scenes', these relations are further elaborated through the bringing together of pedigrees into the family file, the creation of the master pedigree, and the movement, location, testing and comparison of material objects – medical records, correspondence, laboratory test results, blood, tissue and DNA samples are identified, accessed, verified and linked.

The enhanced sense of biological relatedness produced in clinical genetics practice as a result of being identified as a member of an at-risk family is not always benign. In the early 1990s, Lippman and others argued that the development of the 'new genetics' and the rapid growth of genetic and genomic science had the potential to lead to an increased 'geneticisation' of understandings of health and illness and for such geneticisation to alter 'relationships, commitments and values'.[7] For Lippman this was important because it was possible that, as a result of becoming increasingly aware of their biological relatedness, people might be less likely to notice, take account of, or recognise the value of, other important aspects of their relatedness. Following Lippman, ethnographic and other research has shown that genetics practice and genetic testing may indeed lead to an increasing geneticisation, and medicalisation, of relationality particularly among members of families at risk of genetic disorders and that, in such families, relations can sometimes come to be defined overwhelmingly in terms of the 'genetic inheritance transmitted through reproduction'.[8] For Finkler, the medicalisation of kinship in the context of genetics has, at its most extreme, led to a perception of families and family members as 'toxic',[9] and Featherstone *et al.* have described the transformation of family members into 'risky relations'.[10]

The identification of a genetic mutation or deletion within a kindred can have far-reaching implications for its members. If my own genes suggest that I have a genetic condition, am a 'carrier' for one, or have a heightened risk of developing one, then that has potential consequences for other members of my family. Precisely which members of my family are or might be affected by the genetic disease varies, depending on the biology of the condition and its mode of inheritance … [T]he increasing identification of genetic disease and genetic risk

---

[7] A. Lippman, 'Led (astray) by genetic maps: the cartography of the human genome and health care' (1992) 35 *Social Science and Medicine*, 12, 1469–1476.

[8] K. Finkler, *Experiencing the New Genetics: Family and Kinship on the Medical Frontier* (Philadelphia: University of Pennsylvania Press, 2000), p. 181; J. Dolgin, 'Choice, tradition, and the new genetics: the fragmentation of the ideology of family' (2000) 32 *Connecticut Law Review*, 523–566.

[9] See Finkler, *Experiencing the New Genetics*, p. 196.

[10] See Featherstone *et al.*, *Risky Relations*.

implies a heightened salience of biological relatedness among family members. Kinship becomes increasingly identified with common ancestry, shared genetic material and genetic risks.[11]

Enriched senses of social relatedness

While it seems inevitable, as Lippman argues, that an encounter with genetics services will lead to some degree of geneticisation and medicalisation of kinship relations and a greater awareness of biological connection, it does not necessarily follow that this will in all or even many cases result in a lessening of the importance of relationships, values and commitments of other kinds.[12] Indeed it seems likely, in the light of the discussion in the previous chapter, that the opposite may be the case. Contrasting the impact of clinical genetics with that of reproductive technologies such as preimplantation genetic diagnosis (PGD), Featherstone et al., for example, suggest that whereas in the context of new reproductive technologies there may be a dilution of kinship, in genetics there is the potential for its enrichment and for the emergence of a greater sense of connectedness.[13] In some cases, an encounter with genetics can even have dramatic effects on families leading, for example, to the reuniting of families where relationships have previously broken down.[14] As the process of diagnosis and counselling progresses and the possibility of cascade screening begins to be considered, patients are asked to relate themselves to others in increasingly complex and multi-layered ways. This can lead to an enrichment of relatedness through patients' efforts to contact long-lost relatives and forgotten branches of families, and through conversations with family members and reproductive partners from whom they may have been separated. Awareness of genetic risk can lead to an enhanced sense of moral relatedness,[15] to a sense of location in a set of reciprocal moral relationships with others and while kinships are, in any case, to some extent sustained and transformed by such relations, this can be dramatically foregrounded in the context of genetics.[16] In addition to its role in motivating communication, moral relatedness can also be a significant

---

[11] *Ibid.*, p. vii.

[12] C. Novas and N. Rose, 'Genetic risk and the birth of the somatic individual' (2000) 29 *Economy and Society*, 4, 485–513.

[13] Featherstone *et al.*, *Risky Relations*, p. x.

[14] Finkler, *Experiencing the New Genetics*, pp. 96–99 and see also p. 186.

[15] R. Rapp, *Testing Women, Testing the Fetus: The Social Impact of Amniocentesis in America* (New York and London: Routledge, 2000), p. 309.

[16] Featherstone *et al.*, *Risky Relations*; D. Schneider, *Critique of the Study of Kinship* (Ann Arbor: University of Michigan Press, 1984), p. 100.

factor in why people seek treatment and testing.[17] The identification
of a shared genetic risk, or diagnosis, within a family can sometimes
lead to the development of new forms of relatedness *between* families
such as patient support groups, national and international patient associations, campaigns for greater recognition of people with the disorder,
and drives to raise funds for research.[18]

Just as in the case of biological relatedness, however, an enhanced
sense of social and moral relatedness is not always benign and an
enhanced *sense* of relatedness does not always imply enhanced *relatedness*. It might for example mean an enhanced sense of conflict, separation or of the existence of mistrust, and in this context relatedness can
sometimes be experienced as much as a burden as a benefit.

[K]inship can be mobilized to signify not only specific kinds of connection
and inclusion but also specific kinds of disconnection and exclusion – as well
as the boundary-crossing trickster movements that confound such classifica-
tions. Since relations of power are central to the articulation of such classi-
ficatory boundaries and movements, kinship is also utilized to articulate the
possibilities for social relations of equality, hierarchy, amity, ambivalence, and
violence.[19]

While the family can, at its best, provide an important source of mutual
support and information, the late modern family can also be highly
complex and fragmented.[20] Against this background, the experience of
many probands of being identified both as at risk or affected by an inherited condition and also, at the same time, as a person with unexpected
responsibility for the distribution of information, often bad news, in the
family, can be a particular burden. This burden falls most frequently
on women. For, given the fact that many inherited conditions are identified in relation to reproduction, it is often women who receive both
information about their own risk and responsibility for informing the

---

[17] N. Hallowell, 'Doing the right thing: genetic risk and responsibility' (1999) 21
Sociology of Health and Illness, 5, 597–621.
[18] R. Rapp, D. Heath and K. Taussig, 'Genealogical disease: where heredity, abnor-
mality, biomedical explanation, and family responsibility meet', in S. Franklin and
S. McKinnon (eds.) *Relative Values: Reconfiguring Kinship Studies* (Durham and
London: Duke University Press, 2001), pp. 384–409; C. Novas, 'Genetic advocacy
groups, science and biovalue: creating political economies of hope', in P. Atkinson,
P, Glasner and H. Greenslade, H. (eds.) *New Genetics, New Identities* (London:
Routledge, 2006), pp. 11–27.
[19] S. Franklin and S. McKinnon, 'Relative values: reconfiguring kinship studies', in
S. Franklin and S. McKinnon (eds.) *Relative Values: Reconfiguring Kinship Studies*
(Durham and London: Duke University Press, 2001), p. 15.
[20] Finkler, *Experiencing the New Genetics*, p. 36.

wider family. Relatedness in the context of clinical genetics is gendered, both in biology and in culture.

From the family to 'the families'

The discussion above has begun to illustrate why it is that the family might perhaps be better thought of as the 'families'. The point here is not that the family can be seen in many different complementary or competing ways or from several different angles, but rather that the family is a *multiple object* with many characteristics – including, among others, characteristics both biological and social. The difference between these two ways of understanding the family – as 'a family' or as 'a families' – is morally significant. In the previous chapter, I explored some of the ways in which the conception of the 'patient in the family' and of the genetics professional as 'family practitioner' led, in combination with the material and other practices of day-to-day genetics, to the emergence of these aspects of genetics practice as problematic and to the construction of the family as a complex assemblage of families. In this chapter, building on the discussion in Chapter 2, I explore the ways in which genetics professionals' attempts to work with the family as both biological and social, and in the context of complicated and changing relations within and between such families, can also lead to the sense among genetics professionals that their commitment to the family has become an ethical problem.

(i)   When patients and families want to manage relatedness

One way in which working with families can become ethically problematic for health professionals is where the relationships of care within a family do not map neatly on to the biological (or even the legal) conception of the family. In the context of clinical genetics this can be particularly problematic. In the family described below, for example, care is provided not by the child's biological parent, but by his aunt and cousin.

A mutation was identified in a woman who was a patient of mine (she died two or three years ago). She had a brother and a sister. The patient also had a son aged fourteen. We invited him in for counselling through the GP. When he arrived for his appointment, he came in with his cousin, with no adult company. He also came with no knowledge or understanding of why he was there. He was not very communicative. During the consultation, we tried to contact his dad but with no success. We arranged for the boy to have a 24-hour urine sample test but he didn't turn up for this. Eventually we were contacted by the boy's aunt who said that she was going to come along to appointments with the boy in the future. For us this raised a number of questions. Is it appropriate to allow the aunt to bring him along even though he is not her child? What role should she have in consent? The aunt and the boy do seem to have a good relationship. But we feel that the dad should be involved. But if the only way the patient is going to come to clinic is with the aunt, and if the father is not taking the parental role, should we work with the family as it is? Also, in the longer term, could the aunt be a way of learning something about the family and how best to support it and the best way to communicate with dad?

If the genetics professional is to support families in their attempts to come to terms with the diagnosis, risk and the ongoing support needs of those at risk, this generally means taking families and their support systems seriously and working with the family as it is rather than as it 'should' be. In the case above, the available carers of the child are his aunt and cousin, rather than his biological father. His father is in the picture somewhere – he has not disappeared – but he is not available. Given this, the genetics professionals involved feel that it may well be that the only way to ensure that the child is provided with adequate support over the coming years is to work with the aunt and cousin. While they would prefer to meet the boy with his father, the genetics professionals believe that if they were to refuse to work with the aunt, the boy would disappear and not get access to treatment.[21] Furthermore, the genetics professionals believe that building a trusting relationship with the aunt might provide an important first step towards establishing a relationship with the wider family, which could then lead to the father participating. A significant ethical difficulty with adopting this pragmatic approach, however, is that the biological information revealed by the test, if it goes ahead, will relate not to the aunt but to the patient, his deceased mother and any existing siblings, i.e. not to the family as 'culture' but to the family as 'biology'.

There are some cases where the tensions between the family understood as biology and the family as culture are explicitly contested by patients and their relatives. These include cases in which, in response to the genetics professional's expressed commitment to caring for the wider biological family, patients and families attempt to manage the limits of such commitments or to negotiate these with the geneticist. One way in which they do this is by stipulating, for example, who is to count and who is not to count as a family member. There were hints of this in the previous chapter in the discussion of cases in which patients refused to share information with relatives. In one case this was because

---

[21] I explore the differences and disagreements between different genetics professionals about ethics and practice in Chapter 5.

of a difference of values – one sister believed in access to abortion, the other didn't. In another, however, what appeared to be at stake was not simply an unwillingness to share information with family members because of a difference of values, but an attempt to place limits upon who was to count as a 'family member'. Here is the case again.

A man aged thirty-five was diagnosed with stomach cancer. Two of his siblings had died of it and his mother died of uncontrolled diabetes. He gave blood and consent to share information 'with family'. A test on the sample confirmed the diagnosis. The sister and aunt were told and were very upset. After his death, his sister and aunt contacted the unit and insisted that they did not want information about the condition and risk to be shared with his wife. They said it had no health implications for her, she would gossip and she 'loved a crisis'. They said that they were also concerned about 'marriageability' of the man's youngest brother. But who is a family member? What is the familial status of the wife?

In this interesting case the limits and nature of genetics professionals' commitment to the family of the patient are called into question by the patient's sister and his aunt, who attempt to exclude his wife from their family. For the genetics professionals involved, this situation is ethically problematic for a number of reasons. On the one hand they wish to support the patient's wife, and feel an obligation to inform her about her husband's condition and cause of death. They also however see themselves as having obligations to the broader family because of the medical and social implications for them as biological relatives. For the sister and aunt, the wife has ceased to be a member of the family and has in fact become a threat to it. She is not a biological relative. Their attempt to manage relatedness and family membership within the clinic makes sense within the context of broader cultural practices of kinship, i.e. with the broader reproducibility of the family through the marriageability of its younger members. They want to control the spread of information and want to stop the genetics professionals from telling the wife and also, indirectly, potential relatives that they have cancer in the family because this is felt to threaten the potential for future biological and cultural relatedness (the reproduction of the family).[22] But to respect their wishes would conflict with the genetics professional's obligations to the patient's wife.

Patients and families attempt to manage problematic relationships between the family as culture and as biology in different ways. In some cases, rather than excluding relatives completely, as above, patients or

---

[22] A. Shaw, *Kinship and Continuity: Pakistani Families in Britain* (Amsterdam: Harwood Academic Publishers, 2000).

family members try to manage or contain relatedness by negotiating a partial solution where, for example, they agree to share some information with biological relatives but only in ways that are incomplete. Situations in which this can happen include those where relationships have broken down, e.g. following divorce or separation. Such partial solutions, where there is a willingness to share risk information but unwillingness to participate significantly in the other's sense of identity (or vice versa), can create as many problems as solutions for genetics professionals.[23]

A man was referred to us in the 1960s with an adrenal tumour and a tumour in his thyroid gland. He was clinically diagnosed with an inherited condition. His father died in his forties but his mother was alive and in her sixties. Screening the man at this stage involved blood pressure monitoring, testing for cacitonin levels (an unpleasant test) and an abdominal ultrasound. In 2002 a mutation was identified in the family, making a genetic test possible for the man's wider family. His sister was tested and found not to carry the mutation. The man has a young son by a previous relationship. He has never seen the son because his current partner felt unable to have anything to do with the child. The man wanted information about the condition and about the test to be available for his son however and gave consent for us to try to contact his ex-partner. We contacted the Child Support Agency who said that if we sent a sealed envelope they would forward it. They did this and we got an instant response and several phone calls. The ex-partner wasn't sure about what to tell her son about the fact that they wanted to do a test on him but she was adamant that she didn't want him to know about his father. She proposed two solutions. One was to say that when she was in hospital the previous year they had found something in her and were going to test for this. The second proposed solution was that we pretend that the information and the test was something to do with a sibling of hers, rather than being to do with the boy's father. We weren't happy with either of these proposals. They would both involve the genetics team in deceit and they would both involve testing, or informing, the child in a way which would mean that he did not fully understand. If we told him about the condition and then said that this was a risk in his mother, for example, this may cause unfounded anxiety. In the end we decided to go ahead with the test. I wasn't convinced it was the right thing. We didn't go into real details with the child about what we wanted the blood for. We did say that he might need follow up. There's a 50 per cent chance that he is not a gene carrier so it might not be appropriate to give him loads of information at this stage. We are still waiting for the test result.

Here the patient's ex-partner wishes to facilitate the sharing of information about biology as long as this does not involve opening the door to the re-establishment of the family as culture. She is willing to acknowledge

---

[23] J. Edwards, *Born and Bred: Idioms of Kinship and New Reproductive Technologies in England* (Oxford University Press, 2000), p. 18.

and act on biological connectedness only insofar as it is possible to manage the social dimensions of the relationship. While they might have some sympathy for the ex-partner's position, this case presents difficulties for genetics professionals because going along with her wishes means allowing the child to be tested without properly understanding why. The genetics professionals feel that an adequate understanding of risk and of the reasons for screening in this case requires an accurate, even if partial, understanding of how this risk arose and believe that an adequate understanding of the biological is not possible without some understanding of the social. In the end, despite their reservations, the genetics professionals agreed to carry out the test without a full explanation and were inevitably left with a sense of moral unease and anxiety about the potential implications – both biological and social – of a positive result.

The cases discussed thus far in this chapter have exemplified different ways in which attempts are made by patients and their relatives to manage the limits of the social family in response to the revelation of biological connectedness and risk. There are also cases in which attempts at relationship management go all the way into the biology – cases where what is being resisted is not social relatedness but biological connection, as in the following case.

We have been working with a family in which an HNPCC mutation is known. One of the daughters was recently booked in for a predictive test but when she came in for it she revealed that she was an identical twin. This is an important fact because it means that a test on her would also be a test on her sister. She said that she had spoken to her sister but that she has decided to go ahead alone because her sister is 'facing difficulties' and not in a position to go through this. We told her that if we did the test it would also be a test on her sister and that we'd be reluctant to do it without involving her sister. She went away and came back shortly after saying, 'I am not an identical twin'. The problem for us of course is that this can't be proved either way without a test.

Here, the patient accepts her social relatedness and a certain degree or kind of biological connection, but denies another particularly relevant kind of biological connection. This is an attempt to manage biology. This case is seen to be ethically problematic by the genetics professionals involved because, if the sisters are in fact identical, to carry out the test on the patient would be to carry out a test on her sister without her consent and it might possibly mean that information about 'her result' will be conveyed to her (by her sister) without adequate counselling, support or preparation. But if the twins are not in fact identical, to refuse a test to the patient would be to deny a patient access to important health care information and, in the particular case of HNPCC, also to deny her accurate knowledge about her risk or the possibility of being reassured that she has not inherited the risk – without which she might have unnecessary screening. In addition to exemplifying the ways in which family members sometimes attempt to manage biological relatedness, what this case also illustrates is that attempts to manage relatedness may sometimes be driven by institutional factors such as the policies of clinical genetics units on when and under what conditions an HNPCC test will be made available. In this case, the twin's attempt to manage biological relatedness seems likely to have arisen out of her awareness that there was a connection between the way such relatedness is presented and the genetics service's willingness to provide access to a predictive test.

This is only one of many ways that institutional or policy factors can be influential in attempts to manage kinship – to manage the 'families' – in ways which can sometimes lead to ethical problems for genetics professionals. In the following case for example, the establishment of a certain type of institutionalised social relatedness (adoption) is dependent upon the *exclusion* of a feature of biological relatedness. In this case it is social workers, rather than the patient himself, who wish to manage social relatedness by managing biology.

A sample from a nine-year-old boy in a residential care home was recently sent to our genetics lab by a general practitioner. The boy's mother has a neurological autosomal dominant condition and his father is schizophrenic. Several attempts have been made to adopt the boy out but all potential families have been deterred by the family history. Social workers want the boy tested because if the test results are negative he will be more easily adopted into a new family.

For the genetics professional this kind of case is troubling because while there are strong professional norms against childhood testing for adult-onset conditions, the best interest of the child may well be served by adoption – on the assumption that this may be better than life in residential care.[24] But, even if concerns about testing children for such conditions are set aside, the 'benefits' of the test will only accrue if the result is negative. What are the implications of a positive test result? For *this* child, adoption becomes less likely still. Because this is a dominant condition, there are equal chances of a test making the child's life better or worse, i.e. of a positive or negative test result. But the child's life without the test is perhaps itself also already intolerable – depending on

---

[24] M. Parker, 'Genetic testing in children and young people' (2009) 9 *Familial Cancer*, 1, 15–18.

what one thinks about residential care. Does this justify providing the test? What should the genetics professionals do?

Taken together, the cases described in this section have investigated the ways in which everyday practice in clinical genetics, notably the commitment to working with families both as culture and as biology, can emerge as ethically problematic as a consequence of the ways in which those who are made aware of their biological relatedness, or that of the people who are in their care, resist, manage or deny aspects of their relatedness – whether biological or social. These cases illustrate how the genetics professional's commitment to the family is a commitment to something that is both changing and multiple.

(ii)   Enduring biology

Just as the complexities of connectedness can lead to problems for genetics professionals committed to supporting patients and their families, so too can those of *separation*. In the cases above, this commitment becomes problematic because, in response to an enhanced sense of risk and of biological connection, there is an attempt to separate off – or out – potential family members. In other cases, by contrast, the awareness of risk and of biological connectedness generated by an encounter with clinical genetics occurs in situations where people are *already* separated, but in which ostensibly well-established separations are called into question. This reveals the partial, dynamic and incomplete nature of separation in the context of biological connectedness which is, by contrast, seen to be enduring. One way in which this kind of issue can create ethical problems for genetics professionals is where genetic information is produced which is relevant to biological relatives who have had very little contact with each other, or with genetics services, and where sharing this information consequently involves contacting relatives out of the blue.

Our clinical geneticists have been working with a patient who recently died, aged thirty-eight, of FAP. Although he was divorced at the time of his death the geneticists know, because he expressed a willingness and a concern to share information, that he has an eight-year-old daughter with whom he has had no contact. The geneticists feel that they have a duty to ensure that she and her mother know about the diagnosis, risk and availability of screening. Because it is FAP, the daughter is at 50 per cent risk and screening can start at fourteen. Although there has been no contact for several years, the mother's name and the daughter's name are known and the team also knows both where they live and their GP's contact details. Our worry is about breaking bad news out of the blue and how to deal with this.

An initial concern for genetics professionals in some such cases is how to find out whether or not the potential recipients would be interested in receiving such information. This is not a straightforward or trivial consideration. How might one go about finding out whether a person would like to receive information without thereby disclosing at least the fact that such information exists? In the case under discussion, by contrast with many other conditions, the seriousness of the condition and the importance of sharing information about it, given the availability of screening, mean that the problem for the genetics professionals is not whether or not to disclose but how to break bad news where it is likely to be both unwelcome and has the potential to raise other issues relating to the source of the information.

In the case above, the patient's death means that the sharing of genetic information does not involve the added ethical problems associated with reconnecting people who would prefer to stay separate, as in the case on page 45 above. In many cases, however, the separation between family members, and hence the distinction between the family as biology and as culture, is less clear-cut. This is particularly the case when children are involved, and where the resulting biological interconnections mean that the potential for some degree of continuing interdependence and for the social and the biological to be interwoven persists, often in problematic ways.

I have known about this family for a long time from the paediatric oncologist. The patient that he initially discussed with me is no longer alive. He had had a malignancy when he was ten and finally died of a gastric cancer when he was sixteen. The fact that he had had three tumours and the potential familial implications of this was discussed with his parents. The paediatric oncologist took a sample and, shortly after death, this was sent over to genetics, with the parent's consent. The couple also have another, younger son. He has severe dyspraxia and is at a special school. The parents subsequently divorced and have had no contact for several years. Recently however, the father has turned up with a new partner. They are trying for a child. His new partner is nearly forty and he is forty. They want to know the risk of cancer in future child. My guess is that the likely diagnosis of the child that died is Li-Fraumeni. There is a big family history of cancer but I think the child represented a new mutation – hence the importance of testing. A test on the sample might make it possible to test the father, and hopefully reassure the couple that they are not at serious risk. The availability of the sample means that a test on the sample is possible. The problem for us is that the man does not want to discuss testing of the sample with his ex-wife because he is sure that she would say no because she didn't want him to be happy. Do we have to have consent from both parents? If I test the sample and I find something what should I say to the mother? If a mutation turns up that is not new this will have implications for the other son. I have been thinking about the harms of contacting the mother, and also about the harms if they found out that I hadn't told them. If I test the family I may not find a mutation but this won't rule out Li-Fraumeni Syndrome.

These are situations in which biological connectedness has the potential to cut across social relations 'irrespective of love and choice'[25] and thereby to illuminate or perhaps reanimate what were up until this point either irrelevant, dormant or virtual dimensions of the 'families' and of the master pedigree. This particular case is problematic for genetics professionals for a number of reasons. It is problematic because, no matter how unlikely a mutation in the family is (as opposed to a mutation in only the son), it remains a possibility. As such, the result of the test could have implications for the couple's other son. And even if the result were to show that this was indeed a *de novo* mutation occurring uniquely in the child who died, this information would have the potential to be important to the child's mother in both reassuring her about her family and in relieving anxiety about her other child, who may no longer be at the same risk.[26] The case is also problematic because the father is requesting that the sample be tested without the mother's consent. Should consent be required in order for the test to proceed? There are good reasons, given the above, for requiring her consent. But, would this not be to give her, as the patient asserts it would, an unacceptable veto over his ability to make an informed reproductive choice? Should access to accurate reproductive information depend upon the consent of a third party?

In the context of partial forms of social and biological relatedness such as the kinds described in the cases above, genetics professionals can sometimes end up devising pragmatic 'solutions' which may nonetheless leave them with an enduring sense of moral unease. An example of this is the following case.

I have been working with a 25-year-old woman, who ran away from home at sixteen and doesn't talk to her mother at all. In fact she hates her mother. She was referred to me because by chance she met her younger sister recently and her sister told her that her mother had breast cancer 'when you were very small'. Her sister told her that she needed to go and do something about it because her grandmother also had breast cancer. My patient doesn't feel able to contact her mother – doesn't want to. It is true that on the evidence she presented, she is at high risk but as a clinician the question you need to ask is whether there are any ways of confirming this. I asked her whether she could find out any more information through her sister. She subsequently talked to her sister and found out that, as far as the sister knew, her mum had had lumpectomies but had never had any other treatment – no radiotherapy or chemo. Most women

[25] Finkler, *Experiencing the New Genetics*, p. 182.
[26] The implications of the test result are important because even if a mutation appears to be *de novo* there is a chance that the parents are in fact mosaic for the mutation in their germline and could potentially have another affected child. Given this, the geneticists would normally offer testing to siblings even if the mutation did appear *de novo*.

with young breast cancer don't survive so is there a chance that the information about cancer in the mother isn't correct? It was difficult to know how to proceed. We could have offered the daughter monitoring. We don't feel that we can go directly to cancer registry or records without the mother's consent, though this does depend to some extent on which registry it is because some of them do release. What I did in the end was call the mother's GP and found out that she didn't have breast cancer. I didn't divulge this information to the daughter but I just cast as much doubt as possible until she accepted that it was very unlikely that her mother had had cancer. The problem is in this kind of situation that the individual patient is extremely concerned and you have to manage this and support them.

The unease for the health professional persists for a number of reasons. While the patient appears to be less concerned than she was, this may not in fact be the case. She may simply feel uneasy about expressing anxiety in the face of the health professional's assertion that there is nothing to worry about. But, even if the patient is genuinely reassured, this has been achieved by a deception and by economy with the truth. Moreover, the information on which this reassurance was based was obtained through an examination of relatives' medical records without their consent. This is a solution which enabled the patient to be informed about her biological risk, potentially avoiding years of unnecessary screening and even perhaps prophylactic surgery, and at the same time enabled her to maintain a desired social separation from her mother. Despite this, the genetics professional is left feeling uneasy about the unavailability of any resolution other than one that can feel morally duplicitous.

While in some cases, such as the one above, there is the potential for the care of the patient to be facilitated by some behind-the-scenes work, in others this is not possible. In the following case, for example, a treatment for a life-threatening condition is only possible through the re-establishment of social and biological connections.

A four-year-old boy living with adoptive parents has a life-limiting X-linked condition. It is very rare and not much is known about it. He is very sick and often in hospital. The only chance for his survival is a bone marrow transplant. The father is not around any more and the mother is not compatible. The boy does however have two siblings who are also in care (aged five and six). The boy's social workers want to locate and test the boy's siblings to see whether they could be donors for the first child. There is also the question of whether they are at risk themselves. What should we do? Who should decide?

In this case, exploring the biological compatibility of the child's siblings as potential donors would require direct engagement with the complexities of social relatedness in adoption. And if one of the siblings were indeed to prove compatible and if transplant was to proceed, this would constitute a significant reconstitution of the biological and social family. This case raises questions about the appropriate limits of the obligations associated with biological connectedness. Do we have obligations to those to whom we are biologically connected, whatever the social circumstances? If not, what are the appropriate limits to this and, in the context of adoption, who should decide about this? When, if ever, do health professionals and social workers have an obligation to protect family members, particularly those who are 'vulnerable', from the demands of their families, even where this means that information and potentially life-saving interventions such as screening would become unavailable? When, if ever, should social separation trump biological interdependence? As was seen in the previous chapter, the familial nature of genetic information means that information from one family member can be of real importance in the care and support of another, and in some cases the availability of potentially life-saving interventions can depend on this. In the context of families characterised by separation such interdependence can create pressure to re-establish family connections.[27] This can be difficult for all those involved and, where the potential source of vital information of relevance to the family as a whole, or to family members, is considered by genetics professionals to be a vulnerable person, this can present significant ethical difficulties.

Such issues do not only arise in cases involving children. A reasonably frequent situation in which such concerns also emerge concerns the testing of people with learning disabilities. In such cases, where the person with the learning disability is a potential source of important genetic information, there may be pressure from family members which raises ethical issues regarding competence, the patient's best interests, and the question of how to strike an appropriate balance, if indeed this is itself considered an appropriate aim, between the benefit of the family and the protection of individual patients.

A 35-year-old man was referred to us because his sister was pregnant. He was referred because a diagnosis had been made on him in the past. The sister did not appear to have this condition but it was requested that this be reviewed and a blood sample taken from the man to confirm the diagnosis originally made in him. When the referral letter came to us in clinical genetics the consent on it was signed by the man's father who said he was the man's guardian and was happy for the blood test to be carried out. A telephone call revealed that the man's father was not in fact his guardian and that the man was living

[27] In the concept of a family characterised by separation, I am recognising that people can be related as separated and that this is quite different from being unrelated or for relatedness to have ended or disappeared. In these families, for example, 'being separated' is experienced as a real and present form of relationality.

in a residential care home, had had only one visit in seven years and had been raised by his maternal grandparents who had subsequently died. He had had no contact with [the] father. The man had a severe learning disability, was deaf and had no verbal communication, other than a rudimentary sign language. It was felt by the carers and staff at the home that a blood test would distress him and was not appropriate. The proposed test was not going to be carried out in the patient's own best interest but for the interests of other members of his family – without the information from the test on him a test on the other family members would be less accurate.

Here, against the background of a well-established social separation, a biological connection becomes illuminated and transforms the 'families' into something different. Different aspects and relations become important. The difficulty for the genetics professional in this case is that what the man's relatives want, against a background of social separation, is access to his body. Both the genetics professionals and care staff at the residential care home are clear that the test would not be in their patient's best interest and are reluctant to carry it out. But, as in many of the cases above, this leaves a number of questions unanswered. For example, could there ever be circumstances under which the carrying-out of the test would be the right thing to do? Could there ever be circumstances under which a test could be in the best interests of such a patient? If so, what might those circumstances be?

(iii)   When the family multiplies

In the first set of cases in this chapter, genetics practice was made problematic because patients' attempts to manage or deny kinship in the face of biological risk revealed tensions within the genetics professionals' commitment to caring for families. In the second, cases were presented in which practice was made problematic by the endurance of biological interdependence in socially separated families. While many problems are created by such dividing or divided families, some also arise when families *multiply*, i.e. in situations in which what was presented as a 'single family' starts to be seen as something more complicated. Some of the most difficult situations for health professionals of this type are those in which genetic testing reveals previously unsuspected disjunctions between the social and the biological family such as unsuspected adoption, or misattributed paternity. And these cases further illustrate the ways in which the 'patient in the family' might be better thought of as a patient in 'the families'. These situations are morally troubling for the genetics professional because this information can be of real significance to the counselling, screening and treatment of 'family members' and cannot simply be ignored as an 'incidental finding'. This information can be generated in a number of different ways. In some situations, genetic testing reveals misattributed paternity (or adoption, or both) in previous generations, with implications for a current patient's risk assessment. A good example of this was one of the cases with which this book began. Here is the case again.

A woman who is trying to get pregnant was recently referred to me because she is a member of a family with a history of a serious X-linked disorder. Her cousin is affected. My patient is interested in using preimplantation genetic diagnosis (PGD) to ensure that she doesn't have an affected baby. We didn't have any information about the mutation in the family so we had to carry out a linkage study to assess her risk. This meant looking at samples from a number of other family members. We were talking about a generation of people in their fifties and over. They were all very happy to provide blood samples. When we tested the samples, however, it became clear that one of them had no genetic markers in common with anyone else in the family, suggesting possible adoption, and another showed non-paternity. These results mean that my patient is not at risk of the condition. What should we do? These events were a long time in the past. Is it acceptable to simply tell my patient that there is no risk of the disease in this part of the family or does she need to know that she is adopted? The person concerned is now deceased so it is not possible to go back to them to ask for their consent to share this information. So, we are just left with this and not knowing how to deal with it.

The problem here for the genetics professional is the question of whether it is acceptable to ensure that patients for whom he or she has a duty of care have accurate information about risk, without disclosing information about paternity and adoption. In a case such as the one described above, where the genetics professional considers the possibility of telling the patient that there is 'no risk of disease in this part of the family', if it is possible to provide the patient with accurate health care information without disclosing this additional information, perhaps genetics professionals have no further obligation. In many cases, however, the social and biological are more intertwined than this and it is not possible for the genetics professional to fulfil his or her duty of care to the patient – to provide them with accurate information about risk – without at the same time revealing the gap that has emerged between the family as biology and as culture as a result of the test.

For genetics professionals, by far the most difficult situation of this kind is where a couple come together for reproductive advice arising out of the diagnosis of an inherited disorder.

John and Sarah attend the Genetics Clinic following the diagnosis of an autosomal recessive condition in their newborn baby. The condition is severe and debilitating and there is a high chance that the child will die in the first year.

The gene for this condition has just been mapped and there is a possibility that prenatal diagnosis would be possible in a future pregnancy. John and Sarah give their consent for a blood sample to be taken for DNA extraction, from themselves and their affected child. Molecular analyses of these samples reveal that John is not the biological father of the child. At their first consultation, when the condition was explained to them, they were told that there is a 25 per cent chance that any future baby of theirs will be affected. The carrier frequency for this condition is approximately 1 in 1,000 and thus the chance that John is also a carrier (since he is not the biological father) is in fact negligible. Should the geneticist disclose the finding of non-paternity with the parents when they come back to the clinic as part of their ongoing counselling? Whilst they did not seek information about paternity, it is of direct relevance to their understanding of the probability of an affected child in future pregnancies.[28]

Such cases raise issues about who is the patient. John and Sarah came to the consultation together for information and advice about their reproductive options. The genetics professional owes a duty of care to both members of the couple to provide them with accurate reproductive information. How should this be discharged? There is understandable anxiety about providing this information to the couple, as a couple. It is potentially difficult information and the health professionals may be worried about the possibility of conflict or be concerned that the relationship may break up with implications for other children. Should the information about misattributed paternity be disclosed to Sarah alone in the hope that she will discuss it with John? There is a chance that this information will not be passed on. But perhaps that is Sarah's choice. But should John, should *any* patient, be allowed to leave the consulting room believing himself (and the couple) to have a 25 per cent risk of a seriously disabled child when in fact his (and the couple's) risk is negligible? Of course, genetics professionals cannot always assume that they have privileged insight. The couple may know about the possibility of misattributed paternity. But this cannot be assumed either. Sometimes in such cases, genetics professionals consider 'fudging' this issue by finding a way to let the couple know that they are at negligible risk without disclosing information about paternity. Could the baby have a new mutation? Could it be the result of a laboratory error? But the success of 'fudging' depends on the patients being less than fully informed, i.e. about the low probability that this is in fact an error in the laboratory. A further worry is the 'other family' – another way in which genetics can produce 'two families'. While John and Sarah together are at negligible risk, Sarah and the biological father of the child have a 25 per cent risk

---

[28] See also A. Lucassen and M. Parker, 'Revealing false paternity: some ethical considerations' (2001) 357 *The Lancet*, 1033–1035 for more discussion of the issues presented by this case.

of having a further disabled child. Is this a relationship that is ongoing? Does Sarah need to know where the risk lies? In some cases, for reasons such as these, the fudging option is seriously considered.[29]

But experienced genetics professionals are only too aware that while fudging can seem like an attractive option in the short term, being less than clear about genetic information can itself create significant ethical problems further on along the line, as the following case shows.

I've seen a family – a man who is a single parent and has three children. He is in his 50s and has FAP. Ages ago, when the family were together, they were all tested by linkage but weren't told the results that two of the children weren't his. The youngest was his but the elder two weren't. Recently we rechecked his DNA sample and found the mutation – so we have some new information to give him. So we invited him in for a consultation. It was difficult because during the consultation he kept calling his various children on his mobile phone to talk to them about the results. We decided, in the light of these conversations, that it would be unkind to tell him that the reason why his two eldest are not at risk is because they are not his. So, I offered to test them all. This seemed alright as a solution at the time. Everyone was happy, but the problem is that the eldest son has now been referred for a colonoscopy by an over-enthusiastic GP who thinks he has fallen through the net![30]

In this case, the issues simply cannot be avoided any longer. The fact that the father was not informed about the possibility that two of his children are not biologically related to him at the time of the initial linkage meant that he continued to believe they were at risk. When the test became available and was provided to all of the children, despite the fact that two of them were known not to be at risk, in order to conceal misattributed paternity, the perception of risk was reinforced. If the two children who are not at risk are to be spared a lifetime of pointless intrusive investigations, the GP needs to be told about the absence of risk. But this creates a problem for the GP – how is the GP to explain to the father that there is no need for the colonoscopy after all?

Could some of these problems have been foreseen? The cases above are presented by genetics professionals as revealing previously *unsuspected* information about adoption and misattributed paternity. It is

---

[29] D.C. Wertz, J.C. Fletcher and J.J. Mulvihill, 'Medical geneticists confront ethical dilemmas: cross-cultural comparisons among 18 nations' (1990) 46 *American Journal of Human Genetics*, 1200–1213.

[30] The clinicians could possibly use the original information produced by the linkage in this case but it will not always be the case that discussion of paternity can be avoided. Take the case of John and Sarah above, for example – if the couple were to separate and John was to come back at some future date with a new partner for reproductive advice it would not be possible to provide him with effective counselling and advice without introducing the topic of misattributed paternity.

reasonable to ask, given the nature of genetic relatedness, just how often the possibility of this kind of issue arising might have been predicted. Not all genetic tests have the potential to reveal family structure to be different to that presented but, where it is possible to foresee the possibility of a test revealing misattributed paternity or adoption, even if the risk is small, should genetics professionals be informing patients about the possibility that (some) genetic testing can reveal misattributed paternity (and adoption) in advance of testing? While having certain attractions, this approach is not itself without ethical complexity.

This case concerns a 42-year-old woman from a high-risk cancer family. Her mother had had ovarian cancer. Her paternal grandmother and her great aunt (and other relatives) had also both had breast cancer. Her father had bladder cancer and her maternal grandmother had had pancreatic cancer. The family is Ashkenazi on both sides, but the mutations associated with people of Ashkenazi origin had not been identified in other members of this family. Nevertheless, one possibility in the case of my patient is to test for the Ashkenazi founder mutations. This is what the patient wants. But should the test be carried out? If the result is negative this is not going to reduce her risk in any way that is clinically relevant. And I'm also worried about the implications for the patient's wider family and for her relationship with them if a mutation is found.

In cases such as this, where there is an awareness before testing that there is the potential for adoption or misattributed paternity to be revealed (even if this is in fact unlikely), should the possibility be discussed with the patient in advance? While in the era of 'patient-centred medicine' there are good reasons for believing that such issues, as possible implications of testing, should be discussed, there are also good reasons for thinking carefully before setting out along this path. In the majority of cases, not only would such conversations be likely to be difficult and distressing, they would also be unnecessary. Furthermore, if this policy were known in advance, or if this discussion took place prior to testing, patients who might benefit from genetic testing and subsequent interventions might be put off and lose out on important information, care and support. Such cases embody complex interdependencies between the family as biology and the family as culture.

Shifting commitments to two families

Like those in Chapter 2, the cases discussed here are presented by genetics professionals as ethically problematic. This suggests that, although the commitment to the 'family' is important, it is nevertheless experienced by genetics professionals as a site of significant ethical difficulty. Chapter 2 showed that this is at least in part because of the ways in which the practices of clinical genetics – the construction of the master pedigree and creation of the family file and so on – lead to the emergence of 'the family' as an assemblage of 'families'. That is, as multiple. The discussion in this chapter has further illustrated this multiplicity and its moral significance through an exploration of three ways in which interplay between the family understood on the one hand as biological connectedness and on the other in terms of more or less stable forms of social relatedness has the potential to lead to the emergence of the genetics professional's commitment to 'the family' as an object of ethical concern.

The chapter began with an investigation of situations in which patients or other family members want to manage their relatedness in ways which resist features of biological or social connection considered to be important by genetics professionals. This arises out of the ways in which people – family members, patients and genetics professional alike – see connections and recognise differences.[31]

Ordinary knowledge about genetic connection gives a choice; there might be no choice about recognising the kinship constituted in the genetic connection itself ... but people may or may not make active relationships out of these connections. They may decide to ignore potential links. So fresh connections may or may not ensue: persons can disappear completely from one's life, or never seem to leave it. In valuing or devaluing their relationships, relatives thus become aware of the way they are connected and disconnected.[32]

The chapter went on to explore the ways in which the genetics professional's commitment to the family emerges as an ethical problem in situations in which morally relevant biological connection is seen to endure against a background of social separation – divorce, estrangement, etc. That is, where recognition of genetic risk (or perhaps the unexpected absence of risk) means that biological connections are reanimated despite the efforts of those concerned to maintain previously well-established distance.[33] These cases – for example where a risk identified in one branch of a family is seen to be relevant to people in another, separated, branch – involve situations where, despite efforts to see things otherwise, the family as biology and its perceived moral implications are hard to resist.

Finally the chapter investigated the ways in which morally significant interplay between the genetics professional's commitments to the family

---

[31] Strathern, *After Nature*, pp. 72–73.
[32] M. Strathern, *Kinship, Law and the Unexpected: Relatives Are Always a Surprise* (Cambridge University Press, 2005), p. 26.
[33] Finkler, *Experiencing the New Genetics*, p. 182.

understood as biology and as culture can occur in situations where the family 'multiplies' in unexpected ways, such as in cases where misattributed paternity or unsuspected adoption is revealed. In these cases, what were assumed to be social or biological relations of one kind can be radically transformed into quite different constellations of relations. These 'new' relations often have the potential to transform the genetics professional's commitment to the family into an ethical problem.

Taken together the cases discussed in this chapter reveal familial relatedness to be hybrid,[34] and characterised by the possibility of morally significant movement[35] back and forth between the family understood as biological connectedness and reproductive partnership on the one hand and as social relatedness on the other.[36] The family pedigree has been shown, once again, to be a living, provisional and fluid object in the context of which there can be 'no closure to conceivable relationships'.[37] The family pedigree is neither flat, nor relatively stable object in the ways suggested by the family pedigree diagram in Chapter 2. It is, by contrast, an object which is multiple in a number of different ways. It is *spatially* multiple – for example in cases in which two fathers, one biological and one cultural, occupy the same space on the pedigree and may or may not be known about. It is *temporally* multiple – for example in cases where connections emerge or change across different generations. And it is an object that is *inherently mobile and changing*. Taken together, this multiplicity suggests that different features of the family are morally relevant or irrelevant in different contexts, in different spaces and at different times. Against this background, the genetics professional's commitment to the family is shown inevitably to have the potential to emerge as morally complicated, and to transform the everyday practices of clinical genetics into an ethical problem.

---

[34] D. Schneider, 'Kinship and biology', in A.J. Coale, L.A. Fallers, M. Levy, D. Schneider and S. Tomkins (eds.) *Aspects of the Analysis of Family Structure* (Princeton University Press, 1965), pp. 83–101; S.J. Yanagisako and J.F. Collier, 'Toward a unified analysis of gender and kinship', in J.F. Collier and S.J. Yanagisako (eds.) *Gender and Kinship: Essays Toward a Unified Analysis* (Stanford University Press, 1987), pp. 14–50; Franklin and McKinnon, 'Relative values: reconfiguring kinship studies'; S. Franklin, 'Re-thinking nature-culture: anthropology and the new genetics' (2003) 3 *Anthropological Theory*, 1, 65–85.

[35] The concept of morally significant movement is one that I return to in Chapter 7.

[36] Edwards, *Born and Bred*, p. 28.

[37] Strathern, *After Nature*, p. 84.

4   Reproducing ethics

Paradoxically perhaps, given the familial dimensions of genetics practice explored in previous chapters, professional guidelines in clinical genetics are often characterised by a very strong commitment to respect for individual patient autonomy. The United Kingdom's Association of Genetic Nurses and Counsellors, for example, calls upon genetic counsellors to, 'enable clients to make informed independent decisions, free from coercion', and to 'respect the client's personal beliefs and their right to make their own decisions'.[1] For the US National Society of Genetic Counselors, the counsellor–client relationship is 'based upon values of care and respect for the client's autonomy, individuality, welfare and freedom', and its Code of Ethics calls for members to, 'enable their clients to make informed decisions, free of coercion, by providing or illuminating the necessary facts, and clarifying the alternatives and anticipated consequences'.[2]

One reason perhaps for the strength of the genetics profession's commitment to patient autonomy is the central role played by reproductive decision-making in clinical genetics and it may not be entirely coincidental that academic studies which have found clinical genetics practice to be highly autonomy-driven have tended to be those that have taken reproductive decision-making as their primary focus.[3] There are a number of reasons why autonomy may be seen by genetics professionals to be particularly important in the context of reproduction.[4] In

[1] The Code of Ethics of the Association of Genetic Nurses and Counsellors can be found on its website at www.agnc.org.uk/About%20us/codeofethics.htm (accessed 29 July 2011).
[2] The Code of Ethics of the US National Society of Genetic Counselors can be found on its website www.nsgc.org/ (accessed 29 July 2011).
[3] C. Bosk, *All God's Mistakes: Genetic Counseling in a Pediatric Hospital* (University of Chicago Press, 1992), p. xix; D.S. Davis, *Genetic Dilemmas: Reproductive Technology, Parental Choices, and Children's Futures* (New York: Routledge, 2001), p. 12; B. Katz-Rothman, *The Tentative Pregnancy* (New York: W.W. Norton and Company, 1986), pp. 49–85.
[4] Clearly context is going to be an important factor in determining the extent to which autonomy is emphasised, in practice, in relation to reproductive decision-making, and

her research for *The Tentative Pregnancy*, for example, Barbara Katz-Rothman found that the main reason given by genetic counsellors in the USA for placing great emphasis on patient-centredness in the context of reproductive decision-making was a combination of the intensely personal nature of such decisions and that, in the end, it is primarily women themselves who live with the consequences.[5] The fact that decisions made in the context of reproductive testing can have implications for the patient's relatives – who the clinician may not have met – can also sometimes be seen by genetics professionals as a good reason for believing patients to be in the best position to make a judgement about how best to proceed.[6] For genetics professionals themselves, the commitment to patient autonomy also reflects a desire to dissociate the provision of genetic counselling from eugenics,[7] commodification[8] and the promotion of abortion.[9]

One of my main aims when I began writing this book was to explore the ways in which the moral commitments held by genetics professionals can come to be seen by them as ethically problematic in the context of their day-to-day practice. What has become increasingly apparent as the discussion has progressed, however, is that it is frequently the everyday practices of clinical genetics themselves – such as, for example, the creation of the 'families' in the master pedigree – which have the potential to create ethical problems around the moral commitments of genetics professionals. Against this background, and building on these earlier discussions, the aim of this chapter is to investigate the various interconnected ways in which the practices of informed consent, non-directiveness and value-neutrality can create ethical problems around the genetics professional's moral commitment to patient-centredness – taking the context of reproductive decision-making as its focus. Before going on to explore the ways in which the commitment to patient-

---

autonomy is likely to be seen as more or less important in different settings. The fact that my focus in this book is on practices in the United Kingdom is relevant here, but as will become apparent in this chapter and the next, there is a great deal of diversity even within this single setting.

[5] Katz-Rothman, *The Tentative Pregnancy*, pp. 22–48.

[6] Davis, *Genetic Dilemmas*.

[7] S.C. Reed, 'A short history of genetic counselling' (1971) 21 *Social Biology*, 4, 332–339.

[8] Davis, *Genetic Dilemmas*, pp. 13–15; A. Kerr, S. Cunningham-Burley and A. Amos, 'Eugenics and the new genetics in Britain: examining contemporary professionals' accounts' (1998) 23 *Science, Technology and Human Values*, 2, 175–198; Reed, 'A short history of genetic counselling'; R. Wachbroit and D. Wasserman, 'Patient autonomy and value-neutrality in nondirective genetic counselling' (1995) 6 *Stanford Law and Policy Review*, 2, 103–111.

[9] Davis, *Genetic Dilemmas*.

centredness can emerge as ethically problematic through an investigation of particular cases, it is important to say something about how this commitment has come about, what it requires of genetics professionals in practice and some of the practical challenges it is seen to present.

Patient-centredness

The concept of 'valid consent' is central to patient-centred medicine. To be valid, consent to – or refusal of – medical interventions such as genetic tests must be informed, voluntary and competent.[10] In the context of clinical genetics, the genetics professional's commitment to patient-centred practice and valid consent tends to manifest itself in: (i) an emphasis on providing patients with all relevant information in a way that is supportive, accessible and understandable; (ii) the adoption of a non-directive approach to counselling; and (iii) a commitment to value-neutrality. Each of these three interwoven strands in the commitment to patient-centredness is inevitably complicated, as are the relationships between them.

(i)   The provision of information

For patients to be in a position to make decisions about their health care and about whether or not to proceed with a particular treatment or intervention, they need to have been provided with and to have understood relevant information. For this reason, the provision of information is at the heart of good, patient-centred, practice in genetics, and genetic counselling is seen at least in part as a process by which patients at risk of a disorder are 'advised of the consequences of the disorder, the probability of developing or transmitting it and the ways in which this may be prevented, avoided or ameliorated'.[11] The patient-centred practitioner is 'aware that individuals have differing preferences with regard to the amount of genetic information they receive at different stages of diagnosis and care',[12] and sees the use of judgement in the provision of information as central to good patient-centred practice.

---

[10] R. Faden and T. Beauchamp, *A History and Theory of Informed Consent* (Oxford University Press, 1986), pp. 274–381.

[11] P. Harper, *Practical Genetic Counselling*, sixth edition (London: Edward Arnold, 2004), pp. 3–4.

[12] S. Burke, C. Bennett, J. Bedward and P. Fardon, *The Experiences and Preferences of People Receiving Genetic Information from Healthcare Professionals* (Birmingham: NHS National Genetics Education and Development Centre, 2007), p. 41.

While fully committed to 'informed choice' genetics professionals know that it can be difficult to achieve in practice.[13] The proliferation of choices and available options, combined with the dynamic nature of practice, means that the array of information is often bewildering and confusing[14] for patients and this can be compounded by the fact that genetic information often needs to be discussed at a difficult and distressing time[15] and because key concepts can be difficult to understand.[16] These challenges can be more difficult still in contexts where there is the need for the use of translators.[17] Lack of resources, notably time to spend on making sure that the patient has understood, can also present an important challenge.[18] Because genetic testing and the provision of information about genetics is increasingly taking place in specialties other than clinical genetics, worries have emerged among genetics professionals that those carrying out this task may not have had adequate training in counselling.[19]

(ii) Non-directiveness

Like the commitment to providing patients with relevant information in an accessible and understandable form, the commitment to 'non-directiveness' is well established in genetics practice and in particular in the area of prenatal testing and reproductive choice[20] where it has become something of a 'universal norm'.[21]

[I]t is not the duty of a doctor to dictate the lives of others, but to ensure that individuals have the facts to enable them to make their own decisions.[22]

---

[13] C. Williams, P. Alderson and B. Farsides, 'Too many choices? Hospital and community staff reflect on the future of prenatal testing' (2002) 55 *Social Science and Medicine*, 743–753.

[14] C. Williams, 'Framing the fetus in medical work: rituals and practices' (2005) 60 *Social Science and Medicine*, 2085–2095.

[15] Burke *et al.*, *The Experiences and Preferences of People Receiving Genetic Information*, p. 24.

[16] *Ibid.*, p. 41.

[17] Rapp, *Testing Women, Testing the Fetus*, pp. 80–86.

[18] Williams, 'Framing the fetus', pp. 2085–2095.

[19] Harper, *Practical Genetic Counselling*, p. 111.

[20] C. Williams, P. Alderson and B. Farsides, 'Is nondirectiveness possible within the context of antenatal screening and testing?' (2002) 54 *Social Science and Medicine*, 339–347.

[21] B. Burke and A. Kolker, 'Directiveness in prenatal genetics counselling' (1994) 22 *Women and Health*, 31–53; A. Clarke, 'The process of genetic counselling: beyond nondirectiveness', in P. Harper and A. Clarke, *Genetics, Society and Clinical Practice* (Oxford: Bios Scientific Publishing, 1997), pp. 179–200.

[22] Harper, *Practical Genetic Counselling*, p. 15.

Why is this? Angus Clarke identifies four main reasons underpinning genetics professionals' commitment to non-directiveness: the value they place on respect for autonomy (especially in the very personal area of reproductive choice); the importance they place on dissociating genetic counselling from eugenics;[23] the need to protect genetic counsellors from their feelings when clients make choices with which they disagree, through the emotional distance non-directiveness makes possible; and the desire to avoid legal accountability for the decisions women make.[24]

Despite their commitment to the principle, genetics professionals acknowledge that it is difficult to be non-directive in practice[25] and recognise that they do influence, even if inadvertently, the decisions made by their clients.[26] The way in which genetic information, for example information about risks, is presented (framed) is well known to have effects upon the decisions people make with that information, as can the incautious use of ambiguous terminology.[27] For this reason, guidelines tend to place a great deal of emphasis on the importance of genetics professionals thinking carefully about the potential impact upon decision-making of the ways in which information is presented.

Genetic information should be given without bias or judgement. Healthcare professionals should be mindful and sensitive of their use of genetic terminology, in particular recognising the impact of terms such as 'risk' and 'mutant'.[28]

In addition to the ways in which information is presented, the choice about what information to include or exclude inevitably has a directive effect – by ruling certain options out and others in.[29] For example, just as a decision not to discuss certain aspects of disability, e.g. disability rights perspectives or the positive experiences of parents of children with impairments has the potential to affect choices made,[30] so too might a decision not to provide information about the existence

---

[23] Reed, 'A short history of genetic counselling'.

[24] Clarke, 'The process of genetic counselling'.

[25] Harper, *Practical Genetic Counselling*, p. 16; Williams, Alderson and Farsides, 'Is non-directiveness possible'; Katz-Rothman, *The Tentative Pregnancy*, pp. 22–48.

[26] S. Cunningham-Burley and A. Kerr, 'Defining the "social": towards an understanding of scientific and medical discourses on the social aspects of the new genetics' (1999) 21 *Sociology of Health and Illness*, 647–668; Williams, 'Framing the fetus'.

[27] Harper, *Practical Genetic Counselling*, p. 16; Rapp, *Testing Women, Testing the Fetus*, pp. 68–71.

[28] Burke *et al.*, *The Experiences and Preferences of People Receiving Genetic Information*.

[29] Williams, Alderson and Farsides, 'Is nondirectiveness possible'.

[30] T. Shakespeare, *Disability Rights and Wrongs* (London: Routledge, 2006), p. 100; Williams, 'Framing the fetus'; Clarke, 'The process of genetic counselling', p. 185.

of discrimination or the lack of support available for people with impairments and their families.[31]

There is also evidence that in some situations simply being offered testing or screening may make it difficult for patients to refuse.[32] Partly this may be because of the unequal power relations between health professionals and patients[33] but it may also be because the offer of screening can itself be perceived by patients to be a recommendation.[34] There is some evidence that strong institutional support is a good predictor of the extent to which women accept testing[35] and this suggests that the way screening is presented and the institutional context in which it is offered affect not only patients' decisions about screening or testing but also their understanding of its meaning and purpose.[36] Relatedly, there is evidence that the rapid expansion of screening in pregnancy and its increasing routinisation may have the effect of undermining choice to some extent.[37] Seeing screening as 'normal' may be directive,[38] and make the 'rituals' of testing and screening difficult to resist.[39] The routine and rather ritualistic nature and manner of presentation may mean that people reflect less on the ethical issues associated with important reproductive decisions than they would otherwise do.[40] In this context, where technology can develop a momentum of its own,[41] it is important to remember that the relationship between technology and choice is one which might be characterised as *co-productive*. The development and implementation of a technology can for example lead to the production

---

[31] Clarke, 'The process of genetic counselling', p. 183.

[32] Williams, 'Framing the fetus'.

[33] M. Stacey, 'The new genetics: a feminist view', in T. Marteau and M. Richards (eds.) *The Troubled Helix* (Cambridge University Press, 1996), pp. 331–349; A. Kerr and S. Cunningham-Burley, 'On ambivalence and risk: reflexive modernity and the new human genetics' (2000) 34 *Sociology*, 2, 283–304.

[34] N. Press and C.H. Browner, 'Why women say yes to prenatal diagnosis' (1997) 45 *Social Science and Medicine*, 7, 979–989.

[35] *Ibid.*; Human Genetics Commission, *Making Babies: Reproductive Decisions and Genetic Technologies* (London: UK Department of Health, 2006); Clarke, 'The process of genetic counselling', p. 181.

[36] Press and Browner, 'Why women say yes to prenatal diagnosis'.

[37] Williams, Alderson and Farsides, 'Is nondirectiveness possible'.

[38] *Ibid.*; Shakespeare, *Disability Rights and Wrongs*; Human Genetics Commission, *Making Babies*, para. 3.29.

[39] A. Lippman, 'The genetic construction of prenatal testing: choice, consent or conformity for women?', in K. Rothenberg and F. Thomsen (eds.) *Women and Prenatal Testing* (Ohio State University Press, 1991), pp. 9–34.

[40] Press and Browner, 'Why women say yes to prenatal diagnosis', p. 988.

[41] N. Brown, B. Rappert and A. Webster, 'Introducing contested futures: from looking into the future to looking at the future', in N. Brown, N. Rappert and A. Webster, *Contested Futures: A Sociology of Prospective Technoscience* (Aldershot: Ashgate, 2000), pp. 3–20.

of particular types of knowledge, in this case of the fetus and the pregnancy, with normative implications for the kinds of decisions people make.[42]

In addition to the routinisation of prenatal testing and screening, women's choices about whether or not to take a test, and about what to do following a positive test result, can be influenced by what they experience as the clear – even if unspoken – assumption that they will terminate an affected pregnancy.[43] The very existence of a screening programme or the availability of a testing technology can lead to the perception that this is the case.[44] For women who have no intention of terminating an affected pregnancy, perhaps because they are against abortion or because they see a child with an impairment as an acceptable even if unsought outcome of their pregnancy, or who are uncertain about what they would do following a 'positive' test result, these assumptions, even if unspoken, have the potential to be experienced as directive – as can the implicit assumption that women who don't terminate such pregnancies will come to be seen as 'responsible'.[45]

In addition to these indirect constraints on non-directiveness, there are inevitably some situations where, despite the genetic counsellor's best efforts, patients' experience of counselling has been that it is explicitly directive.[46] And, while it is likely to be uncommon in practice, some patients do report having been given explicit advice to terminate an affected pregnancy.[47] The possibility of non-directiveness is in practice also inevitably limited by structural factors. Genetics services operate, for example, within certain legal and economic constraints – the law on termination of pregnancy (of which more later) being one of them and the budgets available for clinical services another.[48] The possibility of non-directiveness can also be affected by social attitudes

[42] M. Michaels and L. Morgan, 'Introduction: the fetal imperative', in L. Morgan and M. Michaels (eds.) *Fetal Subjects, Feminist Positions* (Philadelphia: University of Pennsylvania Press, 1999), pp. 1–10; Williams, 'Framing the fetus'; Press and Browner, 'Why women say yes to prenatal diagnosis'; Katz-Rothman, *The Tentative Pregnancy.*

[43] A. Clarke, *Genetic Counselling: Practice and Principles* (London: Routledge, 1994), p. 18.

[44] Human Genetics Commission, *Making Babies*, para. 3.15.

[45] T. Marteau and H. Drake, 'Attributions for disability: the influence of genetic screening' (1995) 40 *Social Science and Medicine*, 1127–1132; Clarke, *Genetic Counselling: Practice and Principles*, p. 18.

[46] Shakespeare, *Disability Rights and Wrongs*, p. 101.

[47] M. Konrad, *Narrating the New Predictive Genetics* (Cambridge University Press, 2005) pp. 130–131.

[48] A. Clarke, 'Outcomes and process in genetic counselling', in, P. Harper and A. Clarke, *Genetics, Society and Clinical Practice* (Oxford: Bios Scientific Publishing, 1997), pp. 165–178; Kerr and Cunningham-Burley, 'On ambivalence and risk'.

such as those towards disability. Overly rigid views about what is 'normal', combined with a lack of real support for people with impairments, can make it very difficult for people to make the choice to continue a pregnancy which is known to be affected.[49] Taken together, these considerations suggest that the boundary between directiveness and non-directiveness may not be clear-cut[50] and this can make it difficult for genetics professionals to ensure that patients are making voluntary/uncoerced choices.[51] This means that genetic testing, although it tends to be presented as offering increased choices, can in fact sometimes limit choice for some women.[52] Such difficulties may be compounded where prenatal testing is carried out by practitioners who are neither necessarily committed to non-directiveness nor adequately trained in non-directive counselling.[53,54]

(iii)   Value-neutrality

The third element of the genetics professional's commitment to patient-centredness is embodied in the emphasis they place on 'value-neutrality'.[55]

It is particularly important that couples realize that, in general, there is no 'right' or 'wrong' decision to be made, but that the decision should be the right one for their own particular situation. It is also important that those giving genetic counselling (and those evaluating genetic services) do not judge 'success' or 'failure' in terms of a particular outcome, and that they give support to families whatever their decisions may be.[56]

Counsellors are trained to be value-neutral in their practice.[57] The idea that respect for patient autonomy, and non-directiveness, require value-neutrality is based on four interdependent concerns.[58] The first of these

---

[49] T. Shakespeare, 'Back to the future? New genetics and disabled people' (1995) 44 *Critical Social Policy*, 45, 22–35; Human Genetics Commission, *Making Babies*, para. 3.34; Kerr and Cunningham-Burley, 'On ambivalence and risk'; Clarke, 'Outcomes and process in genetic counselling'.

[50] Kerr, Cunningham-Burley and Amos, 'Eugenics and the new genetics in Britain'; Williams, Alderson and Farsides, 'Is nondirectiveness possible'.

[51] Williams, 'Framing the fetus'; Shakespeare, *Disability Rights and Wrongs*, p. 101.

[52] Rapp, *Testing Women, Testing the Fetus*, p. 37.

[53] Harper, *Practical Genetic Counselling*, p. 111; Clarke, 'The process of genetic counselling'.

[54] The differences between the practices of different professional groups involved in genetics are discussed in Chapter 5.

[55] Rapp, *Testing Women, Testing the Fetus*, p. 59.

[56] Harper, *Practical Genetic Counselling*, p. 16.

[57] Rapp, *Testing Women, Testing the Fetus*, pp. 96–100.

[58] Wachbroit and Wasserman, 'Patient autonomy and value-neutrality'.

is a concern that, were they openly expressed, the genetic counsellor's values might carry undue weight with clients because they would be attributed with an inappropriate degree of scientific or moral weight. The second concern underpinning the commitment to value-neutrality arises out of a worry that, because of the circumstances in which genetic counselling takes place, the autonomy of patients requesting genetic testing may be particularly fragile. Third is a concern, reflected in some of the discussion above, that social pressure on patients faced with making decisions about prenatal testing is especially great. The fourth is a concern that allowing or encouraging the expression of values by health professionals might lead to a slippery slope to coercion or inappropriate paternalism.

Notwithstanding their broad commitment to value-neutrality, some genetics professionals have doubts about the extent to which it is always desirable to practice in a value-neutral way in every case. Are there not some situations in which the expression of values by genetics professionals might form an important part of good – patient-centred – practice? Might there not be circumstances under which the expression of genetics professionals' values may in fact contribute to the promotion of autonomy?[59] The suggestion here is that respect for autonomy and maintaining value-neutrality might not necessarily always pull in the same direction and that it may as a consequence be a mistake to assume that counsellors' expressions of values must always in every case undermine autonomy.[60] One way in which an (over)emphasis on value-neutrality and non-directiveness might undermine autonomy might for example be where it stifled discussion and reflection.[61]

[I]t may be very helpful to encourage a client to consider the likely consequences for themselves and others of the various decisions they might make (e.g. not to be tested, to be tested and have a favourable result, to be tested and have an unfavourable result). Such encouragement may be seen as being directive, leading the client to consider implications that he/she would not have otherwise confronted. An excessive attachment to non-directiveness could paralyse this counselling component of genetic counselling, in which the confrontation of

---

[59] *Ibid.*; M. Parker, 'Deliberative bioethics', in R.E. Ashcroft, A. Dawson, H. Draper and J. McMillan (eds.) *Principles of Health Care Ethics*, second edition (Chichester: John Wiley and Sons, 2007), pp. 185–191.

[60] Wachbroit and Wasserman, 'Patient autonomy and value-neutrality'; Davis, *Genetic Dilemmas*, p. 21.

[61] Williams, Alderson and Farsides, B. 'Is nondirectiveness possible'; Burke and Kolker, 'Directiveness in prenatal genetics counselling'; A. Caplan, 'Neutrality is not morality: the ethics of genetic counseling', in A. Caplan, B. LeRoy and D. Bartels (eds.) *Prescribing our Future: Ethical Challenges in Genetic Counseling* (New York: Aldine Press, 1993), p. 161.

clients with information or with possible future scenarios may be an essential element.[62]

A second kind of situation in which genetics professionals may take the view that value-neutrality might not be ideally compatible with patient-centredness is where a woman would *prefer* her genetic counsellor to take a more active role. There is evidence that some women facing difficult reproductive decisions value 'appropriate directiveness'[63] and it has been argued that directiveness can sometimes be an important part of helping women who are facing difficult decisions.[64] Where this is the case, rigid adherence to value-neutrality and non-directiveness may go against both the best interests of women and their wishes, i.e. it may not actually be patient-centred.

Choices and problems

Notwithstanding the difficulties associated with its achievement in practice, genetics professionals are strongly committed to the non-directiveness ethos[65] and to patient-centredness more broadly.[66] The previous section has identified three interwoven and interdependent strands in the genetics professional's commitment to patient-centredness: an emphasis on providing patients with all relevant information in a way that is supportive, accessible and understandable; a commitment to the adoption of a non-directive approach to counselling; and an emphasis on the importance of value-neutrality. Building on the discussions in previous chapters, the remainder of this chapter investigates the ways in which the genetics professional's commitment to patient-centredness can be made problematic by the practices of information-giving, non-directiveness and value-neutrality in the context of reproductive decision-making. While the three interwoven strands of the commitment to patient-centredness identified above are woven into and play key roles in the emergence of everyday practice as problematic, it is

---

[62] Clarke, 'The process of genetic counselling'.

[63] Harper, *Practical Genetic Counselling*, p. 16; T. Marteau, H. Drake and M. Bobrow, 'Counselling following diagnosis of a foetal abnormality: the differing approaches of obstetricians, clinical geneticists and genetic nurses' (1994) 31 *Journal of Medical Genetics*, 864–867; Williams, Alderson and Farsides, 'Is nondirectiveness possible'; Rapp, *Testing Women, Testing the Fetus*, p. 60 and pp. 97–98.

[64] Williams, Alderson and Farsides, 'Is nondirectiveness possible'; Clarke, *Genetic Counselling: Practice and Principles*; Burke and Kolker, 'Directiveness in prenatal genetic counselling'.

[65] Clarke, 'The process of genetic counselling'.

[66] R. Chadwick, 'Genetics, choice and responsibility' (1999) 1 *Health, Risk and Society*, 293–300.

important to note at the outset that they do not map directly or neatly onto each of the themes – seriousness, certainty and uncertainty, and selection – that are explored in the discussion which follows.

(i)   Seriousness

One way in which the genetics professional's commitment to patient-centredness can emerge as a problem is where they consider patients to be making reproductive decisions that are mistaken, misguided or immoral.[67] A common example of this is where genetics professionals consider patients' requests for access to prenatal testing and termination of pregnancy to be inappropriate. In the case below, for example, following the finding of an anomaly on a routine screen, a patient requests a termination of pregnancy for what the genetics professional considers to be a 'minor condition'.

One of my patients is a 45-year-old pregnant woman who has been in a relationship with her partner for fifteen years. This is their first pregnancy. She has had an amniocentesis which revealed – as an incidental finding – that the baby has Triple X Syndrome. After discussing it with her partner, my patient has told me that she has decided to terminate the pregnancy. I find it really hard to reconcile her request for termination with a reasonably positive prognosis for Triple X. Most girls with Triple X look normal and go to normal schools. They are fertile and have normal babies. But even though we have talked it over and they have had time to think about their options, my patient and her partner see it as a major problem – especially the possibility of development delay. I see it as my job to tell them what we know about prognosis whilst at the same time being respectful. But is it my job to challenge their decision if I think it is wrong? I'm not sure. My reading of the more recent literature is that it suggests an even milder phenotype than I'd previously thought. I'm not sure what I should do.

Although the genetics professional here is strongly committed to supporting the reproductive choices of her patient, she is nevertheless concerned about the decision to terminate the pregnancy. One reason for her concern arises out of a worry about the possibility that this decision may be being made on the basis of a misunderstanding about the 'seriousness' of Triple X and its implications. In the context of what is a much-wanted pregnancy, the decision to opt for a termination of pregnancy because of a condition with a generally very mild phenotype seems to the genetics professional to be a mistake. There is among

---

[67] Some examples of this outside of the context of reproductive choice were also discussed in Chapter 2, for example those in which genetics professionals were concerned because patients refused to share important information with their relatives.

other things a worry here that her patient's advanced reproductive age may rule out subsequent pregnancies and that, as a consequence, the decision to terminate might be one she will come to regret. What are the genetics professional's obligations in this case? Having discussed this issue with the couple and given them time to think about the decision for themselves, she wonders whether she should now take their choice at face value or whether she ought to challenge this decision further. She feels torn between her commitment to non-directiveness on the one hand and her commitment to well-rounded patient choice – which seems in this case to call for further challenge – on the other. Some degree of challenge seems appropriate in this case, but what form should this take?

For some genetics professionals, over and above the question of whether the decision is adequately informed or genuinely reflects the patient's values, there is a concern about whether acting on the patient's wishes would be compatible with the goals of clinical genetics. For these genetics professionals, whatever their views about the availability of abortion more broadly, the primary role of the genetics service should be to help those at risk of serious inherited disorders. What this means is, that for genetics professionals, the concern presented by this kind of case is one about the appropriateness of termination of pregnancy – within the context of clinical genetics – for what the genetics professional considers to be a 'minor condition'. In the case above, for example, while it is true that girls with Triple X may have slightly lower intelligence than their siblings and be at some risk of mild speech and development delay, they are in most cases completely unaware of their karyotype, as are those around them. They have normal appearance, their sexual development and puberty are normal and they go on to have chromosomally normal babies.[68] For many genetics professionals, this is not the kind of prognosis which justifies terminating a wanted pregnancy – in the context of a genetics service. In such situations they are torn between their fundamental commitment to patient-centredness on the one hand, and their view, on the other, that the role of the clinical genetics service is to provide a service – including termination of pregnancy where appropriate – to those at risk of serious inherited disorders, i.e. that they are not a termination of pregnancy service.

While, in the case above, the ethical problem has its origins in an incidental finding from a relatively routine amniocentesis carried out

[68] H.V. Firth and J.A. Hurst, *Oxford Desk Reference: Clinical Genetics* (Oxford University Press, 2005), p. 494.

because of the pregnant woman's age,[69] the most common situation in which the question of how to deal with information about minor conditions arises is in the context of a request by a pregnant patient for a prenatal test. In these situations the question is, at first glance, one about whether prenatal testing is appropriate rather than about termination of pregnancy. In practice, however, prenatal testing – by contrast with routine screening – is only usually considered appropriate where there is a view that termination of an affected pregnancy is likely to follow.[70] And, because of this, requests by patients for prenatal testing for 'minor' conditions can also – like requests for termination of pregnancy – sometimes present a challenge to the genetics professional's commitment to patient-centredness.

An issue that is important for many of us is when someone wants a prenatal test … for what we think of as a minor condition. So, very few people would have difficulties with an anencephalic fetus, not compatible with life, but we face situations that are perfectly compatible. Three difficult ones for me have been Charcot-Marie-Tooth, Neurofibromatosis type 1 and Alport's Syndrome.

In the context of a request for prenatal testing by women who want to have a child, one concern is that prenatal testing presents a small but not insignificant risk of miscarriage. This means that genetics professionals may be concerned that the patient who requests this for a minor condition has not fully understood the nature of the risk and its importance in the context of a wanted pregnancy or that, if they have understood it, they may not be weighing it appropriately against a concern about the condition for which the test would be carried out.[71] Just as with requests for termination of pregnancy after a routine screen such as in the case discussed above, however, many genetics professionals consider prenatal testing (and possible termination of pregnancy) to be inappropriate in the context of minor conditions even if the woman herself sees this as something which is of sufficient concern to outweigh any worries she might have about the risk of miscarriage. For these reasons, many genetics professionals are unhappy about providing such testing.

---

[69] In this respect, this case exemplifies the point made earlier in this chapter – in the section on 'non-directiveness' – about the ways in which routine screening has the potential to generate unforeseen issues.

[70] This connection and its appropriateness will be discussed in more depth in the next section, on the role of 'certainty'.

[71] This risk is likely to be reduced if not disappear altogether as less invasive forms of prenatal testing using maternal blood are developed and introduced into day-to-day practice.

Not all genetics professionals take this view of course. For many, despite their reservations about prenatal testing and termination for minor conditions, the choice is one to be made by the woman herself on the basis of her own values. But, whatever their own views about the importance of reproductive autonomy in genetics, the extent to which genetics professionals are free to adopt a strongly patient-centred approach in the area of reproductive medicine, that is, to be non-directive and value-neutral in their support for women making decisions about termination of pregnancy, is inevitably circumscribed by the relevant law on abortion. In the United Kingdom, for example, abortion is legal at any point up until term, 'if two registered medical practitioners are of the opinion, formed in good faith ... that there is a substantial risk that if the child were born it would suffer from such physical or mental abnormality as to be seriously handicapped',[72] that the termination is necessary to prevent 'grave permanent injury to the physical or mental health of the pregnant woman',[73] or that 'the continuance of the pregnancy would involve risk to the life of the pregnant woman, greater than if the pregnancy were terminated'.[74] At or below twenty-four weeks, termination of pregnancy is also permissible where two registered medical practitioners are of the opinion, again 'formed in good faith' that, 'the continuance of the pregnancy would involve risk, greater than if the pregnancy were terminated, of injury to the physical or mental health of the pregnant woman or any existing children of her family'.[75] What this means is that before twenty-four weeks – when most decisions about prenatal testing and termination of pregnancy take place – the relevant criteria are: (i) substantial risk of serious handicap; (ii) risk of grave permanent injury to the physical or mental health of the woman; (iii) risk to the life of the woman greater than if the pregnancy were terminated; or (iv) a judgement that the continuance of the pregnancy would involve risk of injury to the physical or mental health to the woman or other children of her family greater than if the pregnancy were terminated. In practice therefore, in the kinds of cases discussed above, the genetics professional's commitment to patient-centredness in the question of

---

[72] Abortion Act 1967, Section 1(1)(d) (as amended by the Human Fertilisation and Embryology Act 1990); information about abortion law and practice guidelines in the USA can be found on the website of the American Congress of Obstetricians and Gynecologists at www.acog.org/ (accessed 29 July 2011).

[73] Abortion Act 1967, Section 1(1)(b) (as amended by the Human Fertilisation and Embryology Act 1990).

[74] Abortion Act 1967, Section 1(1)(c) (as amended by the Human Fertilisation and Embryology Act 1990).

[75] Abortion Act 1967, Section 1(1)(a) (as amended by the Human Fertilisation and Embryology Act 1990).

access to termination of pregnancy is circumscribed by the requirement either that there is a substantial risk of 'serious handicap' or that the continuance of the pregnancy would involve risk to the mental health of the woman greater than were the pregnancy to be terminated.

In many areas of medicine, for example in general practice, it is the second of these criteria which is most often relevant to decisions about the appropriateness of access to termination of pregnancy – where, for example, a woman who is unexpectedly pregnant approaches her general practitioner for a termination. Against this background, an important practical question for genetics professionals is whether the principles by which decisions about access to termination of pregnancy are guided in clinical genetics ought to be the same as elsewhere in medicine. At first glance, there may seem to be good reasons for believing that they should be different. For while the woman who visits her general practitioner may do so because she is concerned about the implications of having a child per se, in the context of clinical genetics the rationale for the referral and hence – it might be argued – for the use of prenatal testing and termination of pregnancy arises out of a concern about whether or not a 'wanted' pregnancy is at risk of a serious inherited disorder. The fact that women, if they meet the relevant criteria, can access termination of pregnancy via their general practitioner might, at first glance, imply that the grounds for decisions about termination of pregnancy in clinical genetics ought to be focused – differently – on the question of whether there is a substantial risk of serious handicap in any resulting child. This position is likely to be untenable for a number of different reasons, however. First, even if it were to be agreed that the purpose of the clinical genetics service was primarily to work with patients and families at significant risk of serious inherited disorders, the question of whether or not a particular patient or their offspring was in fact at risk of such a disorder would not always be answerable definitively prior to a referral. The nature of many inherited disorders is such that their accurate diagnosis requires the skills and experience of the clinical genetics team. While a person may be appropriately assessed to be at risk at the time of referral – based perhaps on their family history – it may turn out on further investigation that they are either not in fact at risk, that their risk status is uncertain, or that the diagnosis is different to that identified at the time of referral. The fact that a person's risk status and the seriousness of the condition from which they are at risk can change as a result of an encounter with clinical genetics services means that it is unrealistic in practice to require that all reproductive decisions other than those concerning serious inherited conditions are managed outside clinical genetics. Second, and relatedly, the distinction between a 'wanted' and an 'unwanted' pregnancy is not going to correspond neatly with professional or institutional boundaries. One obvious factor here is that, for many women whose pregnancy is potentially at risk of an inherited disorder, the question of whether or not the pregnancy is 'wanted' will be greatly influenced by information – potentially from a prenatal test or from a consultation with a genetic counsellor – about the pregnancy's risk status. Third, and related to the previous two points, in addition to the ambiguity or uncertainty of risk status at the time of referral, the marking of a clear distinction between serious and minor conditions as a way of deciding what is and is not appropriate reproductive practice in clinical genetics is likely to be made difficult in practice by the fact that what counts as a substantial risk of serious handicap is something about which there can be reasonable disagreement – clinically, between clinicians and patients, and between family members. Furthermore, just as risk status may change through the process of genetics counselling and testing so too can views about the seriousness of an impairment, and such disagreement may only become apparent as the process of genetic counselling progresses and as a patient comes to know more about the genetic condition and its implications.

The possibility of reasonable disagreement about seriousness is important for the genetics professional because the commitment to value-neutrality and non-directiveness brings with it a commitment to the idea that seriousness cannot simply be read off from the biological facts. For the patient-centred practitioner the question of what is 'minor' or 'serious' in any particular case must inevitably depend to at least some degree upon the patient's beliefs, values and experiences. However, while it is uncontroversial for the patient-centred practitioner that patient values and patient experience should play a significant role in reproductive decision-making, the view that experience has a role to play in the assessment of seriousness can sometimes be problematic.

One of my patients is a pregnant woman in a BRCA2 family. She had dreadful personal experience of breast cancer at the age of twenty-one. She says that she would like to test her pregnancy and would terminate a gene carrier of either sex because she would like to eradicate the gene from the family if at all possible – doesn't want to be responsible for passing it on. Her experience was so awful that she can't bear this thought. Although I would be ok with terminating 'affected' females, I don't believe that termination of pregnancy would be appropriate for carrier males even though there is some increased risk of adult prostate cancer in them. The team in the lab agree with me on this. My other concern is that my patient has likely got reduced fertility after chemo and may have further cancer. This may mean that she may regret multiple terminations of pregnancies if she remains childless as a result. She wants a child.

Because of her own experience of breast cancer, the woman in this case considers mutations in both female and in male fetuses to be serious. She wants to go further than the avoidance of an affected daughter. She wants to eradicate 'the gene' from her family completely so that 'no one else has to suffer' and sees this as a good reason to detect and terminate both female and male pregnancies carrying the mutation.[76] The problem here for the genetics professionals is that, were the pregnancy carried to term, any resulting male child's own health would be largely unaffected by his BRCA carrier status – its primary implications would be for his reproductive decision-making and for the future health of any female descendants he might go on to have. Because of this the genetics professionals, including the laboratory staff, do not see BRCA carrier status as an appropriate basis for selective termination of male pregnancies even though, for the patient herself, BRCA2 carrier status in boys is 'serious' because of its implications – understood through the prism of her own experience – for her son's daughters or grand-daughters. As in previous cases, there is a tension here between the genetics professional's commitment to patient-centredness and her view about the appropriate use of genetic services. For while the genetics professional sees it as important to take the woman's experience, values and beliefs seriously, the difficult practical ethical question she is faced with is just how much weight should be given to such experience in the assessment of seriousness and in the appropriateness of prenatal testing. How is she to make sense of the discrepancy between her own assessment of the implications of a test result on the one hand, and her patient's assessment on the other?

As well as rendering problematic the question of what it means for a condition to be 'serious', it becomes clear from a consideration of this case and others like it that it is not always going to be easy in practice to disentangle the different legal justifications for termination of pregnancy before twenty-four weeks, i.e. to separate out the question of whether there is substantial risk of 'serious handicap' from the question of whether the continuance of the pregnancy would involve 'risk, greater than if the pregnancy were terminated, of injury to the physical or mental health of the pregnant woman or any existing children of her family'. This is going to be difficult because in some cases the implications of the patient's *perception* of the seriousness of the harm and her concern about this – whatever the genetics professional thinks about this – will be such that the risk of injury to her mental health might reasonably be said to be greater were the pregnancy continued than were it

[76] Kerr and Cunningham-Burley, 'On ambivalence and risk'.

to be terminated. Judgements about the seriousness of the impairment and the 'seriousness' of the impact of the continuance of the pregnancy on the mental health of the woman are sometimes difficult to tease apart. To what extent and when does real anxiety, even if based on what genetics professionals consider a misunderstanding of the implications of the condition, constitute good ethical or legal grounds for providing access to termination of pregnancy within the context of clinical genetics? Inevitably these are not going to be easy questions to answer in practice and are going to further challenge understandings of the role of genetics practice, rendering more problematic still the idea that it might be possible for a clear distinction to be maintained between the principles guiding decisions about access to termination of pregnancy here and those applied elsewhere in medicine.[77]

While these issues can be difficult in cases such as those above involving carrier status or conditions with what the genetics professionals consider to be a 'mild' phenotype, they are tested even more forcefully in cases where, while there is a great deal of anxiety, there is no inherited disorder at all.

A woman with two sons with a sex-linked disease has requested prenatal testing in a third pregnancy. Some people would use prenatal testing and terminate affected pregnancies, some wouldn't. She requested identification and termination of all males even though a test is available that could distinguish boys with and without the condition. She did not want this because she believed that within the context of her family she would find it difficult to cope with an affected or an unaffected son. Psychological difficulties for the healthy son.

In this case, the genetics professional's commitment to patient-centredness is made problematic because the patient wants to use termination of pregnancy to avoid having not only a child with a serious X-linked disorder but also a child in which there is no question of a 'serious' disorder, nor even of carrier status. The patient wishes to select against a male pregnancy – whether affected or not – but would continue a female pregnancy to term irrespective of carrier status. This presents what might perhaps be a limiting case for the discussion of access to prenatal testing and termination of pregnancy for minor conditions. In this case, the question of how much weight should be placed on the views of the woman about whether or not a pregnancy should be terminated is brought into sharp focus, as is the question of what ought to be the appropriate limits to patient-centredness. One possible way forward in this particular case might be to make available a test which would

---

[77] These issues about the role of disciplinary boundaries will be investigated in the following chapter.

only differentiate between affected and unaffected male pregnancies, but if the genetics professional does this and the test reveals the pregnancy to be an unaffected male this might be sufficient to provide the information which would enable the woman to obtain a termination of pregnancy elsewhere. Another possibility might be to do the test but to refuse to disclose anything other than whether or not the pregnancy is an affected male, i.e. not to distinguish between unaffected male and female pregnancies. While the genetics professional may in the end come to the view that this is the right thing to do, in so doing she has moved significantly away from patient-centred practice.

In addition to testing the limits of the extent to which seriousness ought to be understood subjectively, this case also shows that situations can sometimes arise in which the concern is primarily neither about the mental health of the woman nor about the seriousness of the disorder in the fetus but rather about the impact of the continuation of the pregnancy on the wider family. In the phrase, 'risk, greater than if the pregnancy were terminated, of injury to the physical or mental health of the pregnant woman *or any existing children of her family*', the Abortion Act in the United Kingdom allows for the possibility that concern for other children in the family might sometimes constitute a legitimate justification for termination of pregnancy. But, how should this phrase be understood in the context of cases such as the one above and in the context of clinical genetics more broadly? One way of reading this – within the context of clinical genetics – would be to interpret it as saying that termination of pregnancy is permissible where the birth of a child *with a serious inherited disorder* would constitute a 'risk, greater than if the pregnancy were terminated, of injury to the physical or mental health of … any existing children of her family'. But once again this rests on a distinction between serious and minor disorders and between the abortion practices of different medical specialties, i.e. between practice in clinical genetics and elsewhere in medicine where it might be legitimate for a woman with existing children to choose not to continue a pregnancy because of a concern about the impact of an additional child on the wellbeing of existing children without reference to the existence of an impairment, serious or otherwise.

Taken together, the cases discussed in this section have explored some of the ways in which the genetics professional's commitment to patient-centredness in the context of reproductive decision-making can create ethical problems because of the key role played by judgements of and negotiations about 'seriousness'. The potential for reasonable disagreement about what is or is not serious in this context, against the wider background context of abortion law and professional guidelines, means that in particular cases – such as those discussed above – patients, genetics professionals, and others including other health professionals can be brought into relation together in ways which render the every-day and otherwise relatively stable commitment to patient autonomy, and in particular those aspects of this commitment which emphasise the importance of non-directiveness and value-neutrality, as ethically problematic.[78] Such cases also raise difficult questions for genetics professionals about whether it is legitimate – or even required – for their practice to be guided by consideration of the kinds of circumstances in which prenatal testing and termination of pregnancy are inappropriate beyond what is required of them by the law – because of the particular focus of clinical genetics on serious disorders – and, if there is a role for these kinds of considerations, how they might play out in the context of a broad commitment to patient-centred practice and in the relationships between clinical genetics and health care services more generally.[79]

(ii)   Certainty and uncertainty

In the absence of effective interventions for many inherited conditions, informed reproductive choice remains a key tool in the care provided by genetics professionals for patients and their families and there tends to be a close link in practice between decisions about prenatal testing and those about termination of pregnancy. Many patients who have been referred to clinical genetics and who end up opting for a prenatal test do so because they are seeking information to help them decide whether they should continue an existing at-risk pregnancy. While reflecting a connection which is important for many patients and a key tool in genetics practice, the close coupling of prenatal testing and termination of pregnancy has the potential, as was seen in the previous section, to generate ethical problems for genetics professionals because it has the effect of turning decisions about access to prenatal testing into questions about access to abortion and hence – at least sometimes – into questions about 'seriousness'. Thus, in the context of a commitment to patient-centredness, this may nevertheless lead to practice which is not sufficiently sensitive to patient values. For patients whose pregnancy is at risk of a 'minor condition', as has been seen already, the link may mean that practice is unable to take account of the wide range of factors

---

[78] The interactions between different health professionals across institutional and specialty boundaries is discussed in Chapter 5.

[79] Caplan, 'Neutrality is not morality', p. 161; Davis, *Genetic Dilemmas*, pp. 21–22.

they consider relevant to the question of whether or not in any particular case a termination of pregnancy is appropriate. In other cases the assumption of a close link between prenatal testing and abortion may fail to adequately reflect that the patient's acceptance of, or even request for, a prenatal test (or routine screen) cannot always be read off as desire or willingness to terminate an affected pregnancy.[80]

A woman carries a chromosomal translocation. This was picked up because of a finding in her brother who is in his forties and in permanent residential care. The woman has had a previous healthy pregnancy. She refused prenatal testing but did agree to have an anomaly scan (not realising that this could reveal the status of the child) and it showed poor development and a hernia (which could be treated with 60 per cent chance of success). After this she had an amnio which revealed that the fetus has same abnormality as the brother. They were surprised by this series of events and this information. She has very strong religious beliefs and would not consider termination of pregnancy.

One response to these kinds of problems might be to try to find ways of de-coupling decisions about testing and termination thereby making it possible for prenatal testing to be viewed as a way of providing information upon which a range of decisions could subsequently be made rather than as primarily an informational tool for those who are already strongly committed to the termination of an affected pregnancy. This might have a number of advantages and some, such as Barbara Katz-Rothman, have suggested that the separating of the decision to test from the decision to terminate would be a good way to enhance the autonomy of women facing testing.[81] It would, for example, reflect the fact that some women will, as in the case above, choose not to terminate an affected pregnancy. It might also mean that there would be less of a worry about respecting a woman's desire for prenatal testing in the context of minor disorders because it would be acknowledged that the decision about termination of pregnancy would not necessarily depend upon the results of the test alone.[82] However, while the de-coupling of prenatal testing and termination of pregnancy might offer certain advantages, it would not be a solution without its own potential problems for the patient-centred genetics professional. This is exemplified by situations in current practice in which decisions about prenatal testing already have the potential to become separated from those about

---

[80] Press and Browner, 'Why women say yes to prenatal diagnosis', p. 986; Rapp, *Testing Women, Testing the Fetus*, pp. 183–190.

[81] Katz-Rothman, *The Tentative Pregnancy*, p. 44.

[82] Clearly an important factor here and in any decision-making would be the risks of miscarriage associated with prenatal testing. This is likely to be less of an issue in the future as more tests using maternal blood become available.

termination of pregnancy and can, as a consequence, lead in their own way to the emergence of the genetics professional's commitment to patient-centredness as a problem.

A couple came to clinic seven weeks into their first pregnancy. Woman is at 50 per cent risk of Huntington's Disease. Her mother is affected. She has never been into genetics before and so there has been no discussion. During the consultation, my patient revealed that she had made a pact with her brother at the time of her mother's diagnosis that neither of them would ever be tested. She still didn't want a test on herself but wanted to have a test carried out on the fetus. Not sure that they would terminate but wanted the test anyway. We had a discussion with them about concerns about testing if they didn't intend to terminate. But we also admired their honesty. They were engaged and were willing to talk about this seriously. The risk is 25 per cent so there is a better chance of getting good news than bad. Deadline for CVS is ten weeks. At next meeting they said that they had thought about it but still wanted the test. We told them that we had real concerns about the impact on the child if the test result was positive and that our default position is not to test because many adults choose not to know and we wouldn't want to remove the possibility of this choice from the child as an adult. Secondly, we worry that it might affect the relationship between the mother and the child. So they went away and thought about it again. What was the outcome? They decided not to test. This raises the question of how much counselling? How directive to be? We consider this a good outcome but is this just because they did what we would hope for?

Cases such as this, where prenatal testing and termination of pregnancy have the potential to come apart in current practice, are troubling for genetics professionals because although they are strongly committed to respecting the reproductive choices of their adult patients, they are also committed to the view that genetic tests for adult onset conditions should not be carried out on children.[83] Where pregnancies are tested for adult onset conditions and the pregnancy is subsequently carried to term, i.e. where a decision is made not to terminate, a test has in effect been carried out on a child without his or her consent. This is unacceptable for the genetics professional because they are firmly of the view – on the grounds of patient-centredness – that the decision to be tested for an adult onset condition should be made by children themselves when they reach maturity, rather than by their parents before they are born. This is seen as particularly important in situations where there are no interventions available, e.g. in Huntington's Disease, as in the case above, where there is good evidence that, when it comes to it, the majority of at-risk adults tend not to take the test even when it is

---

[83] M. Parker, 'Genetic testing in children and young people' (2009) 9 *Familial Cancer*, 1, 15–18.

offered. This concern about the link between prenatal and childhood testing means that genetics professionals are reluctant to offer prenatal testing in situations where the termination of an affected pregnancy is not being contemplated,[84] or where there is real uncertainty about this. For the genetics professional in such cases, the commitment to patient-centredness emerges as ethically problematic to the extent that there is genuine uncertainty about whether a positive prenatal test result will be followed by a decision to terminate the affected pregnancy, that is, to the extent that this is likely to turn out in fact to have been or not a test on a child. The implication of this is that the greater the uncertainty a patient experiences – or, perhaps, expresses – about whether they will terminate an affected pregnancy, the less likely it is that their desire for a prenatal test will be fulfilled because, for the genetics professional, such uncertainty means that the commitment to patient-centredness pulls in two conflicting directions: the greater the patient's uncertainty about termination, the greater the extent to which the sense of obligation to the possible future child outweighs that to the patient requesting the prenatal test. While the most troubling situations for genetics professionals are those involving a request for a prenatal test for an adult onset condition – because of concerns about childhood testing – similar issues and concerns arise in situations where testing is requested for a condition for which an intervention is available in childhood, e.g. screening in FAP,[85] and in general even though there is no doubt that genetic testing for the condition will need to take place in any resulting child (if the decision is made not to terminate the pregnancy), genetics professionals tend, even here, to take the view that testing should usually not be carried out prenatally.[86]

The majority of cases of this type, in which a request for prenatal testing renders the genetics professional's commitment to patient-centredness ethically problematic, arise because – as in the cases discussed above – there is uncertainty about whether the identification of an inherited disorder through such testing is likely to lead to the termination of the affected pregnancy. In other cases, despite the fact that the decision about termination is not in doubt, the relationships between the commitment to patient-centredness and questions of certainty are

---

[84] Geneticists also worry that if they allow PND without termination of pregnancy this would, on the grounds of consistency, require them to offer testing for existing older children. Similar issues arise in the context of national screening programmes which, as an incidental finding, identify carrier status. Should this carrier status be disclosed to parents? If so, what is the morally significant difference between this and testing older children for carrier status?

[85] Parker, 'Genetic testing in children and young people'.

[86] *Ibid.*

interwoven in quite different but no less complex or ethically problematic ways.

A couple had prenatal testing at thirty-two weeks which revealed the pregnancy to be trisomy 18 (Edwards Syndrome) with complex heart anomalies. Only 10 per cent live to one year. Child also has oesophageal atresia (treatable by surgery). The family have decided not to terminate but do not think it is appropriate to carry out surgery and want to let nature take its course when the child is born. This raises the question of how to deal with the child in the weeks after birth. Lots of distress – also concern that parents might change their mind when they see the child. Should the old or the potential new decision be respected? Not possible to 'keep comfortable' if the atresia makes feeding impossible. Benefits to family of treatment and of longer time together.

Here, the problem is not so much about whether or not the patient's choice not to terminate should be respected as about what is to count as patient-centredness, combined with uncertainty about the ways in which the requirements of patient-centredness might change as the case unfolds. Following a prenatal test, which has revealed the pregnancy to be affected by a serious disability, the couple have decided to continue the pregnancy to term but for life-prolonging treatment to be withheld from the child when he or she is born. The case is complicated by the fact that the distinction between what constitutes life-prolonging treatment on the one hand, and treatment for the relief of the child's suffering on the other, is not an easy one to draw. The surgery that would relieve some of the child's suffering would probably also have the effect of extending the child's life. The situation is complicated still further by the genetics professional's view that the surgery might offer certain benefits if it enabled the parents and the child to have a longer time together. For the genetics professionals involved in this case, the parents' refusal of treatment presents ethical challenges not only in relation to the making of end-of-life decisions in neonates. The various features of this situation also mean that the parents and the genetics professionals – and in the future, other health professionals in neonatal intensive care – are brought together in ways which lead to significant complexity and uncertainty around the question of what constitutes patient-centred practice.

There are other situations within the context of reproductive decision-making, in which the problem facing the patient-centred genetics professional is to work out just what it means to be patient-centred in a particular case.

Husband at direct risk of HD. Couple wanted to start a family. Put off having children but now are aware of developments in technology. Would like to have access to PGD. But man did not want his own status clarified at all. It was apparent to the clinicians that he was already showing signs. I felt that if I referred them for PGD without discussing the signs I would be copping out. Not knowing whether or how to share my concerns about the husband and run the risk of upsetting her. But if I didn't say, I might be risking the possibility of denying her a baby. After much thinking we tried to get them back to the clinic and she came alone. I asked her what she thought and she said she was worried about him. At which point she became absolutely devastated. But I felt that I couldn't live with not having disclosed this information.

Here, within the context of a consultation about access to PGD, information emerges about the husband's health which is relevant to the decision at hand but which has not been explicitly requested and is not the result of a genetic test in the usual sense of the word – the diagnosis is simply *there*. The question of what is patient-centred practice is deeply problematic for the genetics professional here and she struggles not only about *whether* to disclose this information but also *to whom*. After much deliberation, she comes to the conclusion that it is her responsibility to raise this issue with the affected man's partner – who is also, herself, a patient. In the following very similar case, the genetics professional comes to a different view.

Family referred. First child had Down Syndrome. Between the initial referral and their appointment, the family discovered that one of the husband's parents had been diagnosed with HD. When they arrived in the clinic the woman was pregnant again. And the husband clearly had evidence of HD. What does one do? Disclose one's concerns? I decided not to say anything – was I wrong?

Here two health professionals, both strongly committed to patient-centred practice and facing very similar situations, come to different views about the moral implications of incidental information relevant to reproductive decision-making and about the right – patient-centred – way to proceed. While both cases involve reproductive choice and both involve the generation of information about a family member for whom the genetics professional has a duty of care, in neither case is it straightforwardly or unproblematically clear what it might mean to act in a way that is 'patient-centred'. Just as in the earlier cases, in which prenatal testing and termination of pregnancy have the potential to come apart, in these cases too, the genetics professional's commitment to patient-centredness is rendered problematic by the existence of *uncertainty*.

(iii)   Selection

The previous section began with an exploration of some cases involving ethical issues generated by the separation of prenatal testing and termination of pregnancy, where the primary concern was with the implications of prenatal testing for the future autonomy of the child. One way in which prenatal testing and termination of pregnancy can be de-coupled without generating this kind of concern is through the use of preimplantation genetic diagnosis (PGD) to exclude embryos shown to be at risk of such conditions prior to the implantation of unaffected embryos in the woman. The use of PGD means that, where a successful pregnancy results, the child will be free of the condition. While PGD involves a demanding procedure, for some women, such as those with history of multiple terminations or miscarriages, or with a strong desire to avoid terminating a pregnancy, it can nevertheless be an attractive option. Despite its attractions, however, the use of PGD can sometimes generate ethical concerns for patient-centred genetics professionals similar to those arising in prenatal testing. For, even though no termination of pregnancy is involved, genetics professionals can sometimes still have concerns about a request for the use of PGD for 'minor conditions'.

A woman with two children with Retinoschisis wants to know whether she can have funding for PGD. This is a rare X-linked condition that affects vision but the prognosis is not too bad. Although the eyesight of males goes off in their teens, they can still see even if not well enough to drive. The gene has been identified. The woman's father had the condition. She knows about the condition. However in her second child the symptoms were very severe and now she wants to have PDG because she thinks it is better than PND and termination. Already has two children with this condition – minor versus serious conditions – criteria for PGD – using sexing – resources good use of money?

The genetics professional's concern about childhood testing for an inherited disorder is clearly not an issue in such cases. Neither is the concern here one about termination of pregnancy. The fact that genetics professionals are worried about the use of reproductive technologies for the avoidance of 'minor' conditions suggests that in addition to the issues of 'seriousness' and 'certainty', at least part of their concern in such cases – and potentially by implication in the cases which involve terminations too – is about the ethics of *selection*.[87] That is, there is a worry here about whether the use of PGD for the avoidance of – in this case – poor eyesight, or in the earlier case of Triple X (which may result in slightly lower intelligence) is compatible with the goals of clinical genetics which are seen to be primarily about helping people at risk of serious inherited disorders and not about *selection*.[88]

---

[87] E. Parens and A. Asch, 'The disability rights critique of prenatal testing: reflections and recommendations' (2003) 9 *Mental Retardation and Developmental Disabilities Research Reviews*, 1, 40–47.
[88] Parker, 'Genetic testing in children and young people'.

Conclusion

The focus of this chapter has been on the ways in which the practices of informed consent, non-directiveness and value-neutrality can create ethical problems around the genetics professional's commitment to patient-centredness in the context of reproductive decision-making. Because of the ways that genetics professionals, patients, their families and sometimes other health professionals are brought together, these ethical problems tend to cluster around issues of 'seriousness', 'certainty' and 'selection'.

The chapter began with an investigation of situations in which patients request access to prenatal testing and termination of pregnancy for what the genetics professional considers 'minor' – or 'not serious' – conditions. It went on to explore cases in which prenatal testing and termination of pregnancy have the potential to come apart, for example as a result of requests for prenatal testing made by women who have no plans to – or are very uncertain about whether to – terminate an affected pregnancy, and the tensions this uncertainty generates between the patient-centred genetics professional's concern to support the reproductive autonomy of women on the one hand and their concerns about childhood testing on the other. The chapter also investigated situations in which the question of what it might mean to be patient-centred was uncertain. Finally, cases were considered in which ethical problems are generated by requests for access to preimplantation genetic diagnosis for minor conditions and the compatibility of what they consider 'selection' with the goals of clinical genetics.

In conclusion, it is important to highlight the potential for connections between the problems explored here and those discussed in earlier chapters. For it is clear that here too, in the context of reproductive decision-making, the family is never far away, that the care of one patient is always also the care of the patient in the families, that is, the family as multiple. This is exemplified by the second of the two cases with which the introduction to this book began. In that case, a woman's access to preimplantation genetic diagnosis, which she and the genetics professionals responsible for her care believe has the potential to enable her to have a child unaffected by a serious X-linked disorder, is itself dependent upon access to information which can only be obtained through tests on blood samples taken from several of her relatives. The test results, however, which identify a case of misattributed paternity and another of undisclosed adoption, reveal the family to be multiple in ways which radically transform both the nature of the woman's reproductive choice (she is shown to be free of the disease-causing mutation) and the form of 'the families' (different social and biological relationships are illuminated as relevant). This in its turn creates new ethical problems for the genetics professional who is committed to care for the patient in the 'family'.

5 Multi-professional practices

Together the preceding chapters have mapped out a number of recurring and overlapping problems characterised by conflicting values and moral commitments. All of these features of the moral world of the genetics professional are, or can be, interwoven and each of these aspects of clinical genetics is characterised by a co-productive relationship between the established relatively stable practices of day-to-day clinical genetics and the ethical problems encountered by genetics professionals in their pursuit of 'good practice'. Against this background, decisions have nonetheless to be made – genetic counselling must take place, genetic tests must be offered or refused. In the day-to-day practice of genetics, played out across a moral landscape characterised by the tensions, resistances and practices described in Chapters 2, 3 and 4, there is a requirement for genetics professionals – clinical geneticists, genetic counsellors and laboratory staff – as real-world actors in real-world situations to make moral judgements about what is the right thing to do. Even though each of these professionals is likely in her own way to be highly committed to 'good practice' this will inevitably – as has been seen in previous chapters – be a commitment to something contested. Different genetics professionals will often have different views about what constitutes best practice in particular cases. Such decisions are also inevitably made within certain other, sometimes conflicting, constraints. Even though in day-to-day practice genetics professionals do have a lot of scope for independent action, they – and the other health professionals with whom they interact – are also members of clinical teams, professions and institutions, having, for example, been trained in certain ways, and inhabiting different professional contexts permeated by sometimes conflicting institutional and professional norms, commitments, traditions and practices.[1] It is against this backdrop that they and their colleagues have the difficult job of judging (and in so

[1] E. Freidson, *Profession of Medicine: A Sociology of Applied Knowledge* (University of Chicago Press, 1988).

doing, of making) what is good practice in particular situations. This complexity and these tensions suggest a fourth way in which day-to-day practice can create ethical problems, one arising out of the differences between the judgements and interpretations of different individual genetics professionals; between the different professional groups in clinical genetics, i.e. between counsellors, geneticists and laboratory staff; and between genetics professionals and the other health professionals with whom they interact.

Ethics and professions

Thus far in this investigation of ethical problems arising for genetics professionals in their work with patients and families, the figure of the *genetics professional* has itself remained somewhat static and isolated. Taking this figure as its starting point, My aim in this chapter is to complement the earlier analysis with an exploration of the different ways in which genetics professionals are situated within a complicated array of professional relationships and the potential these relationships have to create ethical problems around the commitment to multi-professional practice. Negotiating these relationships is especially important because these professional domains – these groups, interests and spaces – are ones through which the patient and the family move, and through which they and the ethical difficulties that are generated by and ascribed to them, are transformed and reconstituted.

(i)   *Disagreements and difference between individual genetics professionals*

The day-to-day reality of engaging with the tensions that I have been describing in previous chapters means that when a patient is referred to clinical genetics (as a proband, family referral or de facto referral) they can sometimes come to inhabit a liminal space in which competing practices are available and between which judgement is required. Before going on to explore potential differences between professions, it is worth underscoring that different views about the best way to proceed are quite possible, if not likely, between genetics professionals within a single team. The discussion in previous chapters has highlighted many situations in which this can be the case. Such differences might arise for a number of reasons – because of conflicting interpretations of the facts of the case, because genetics professionals place greater or lesser emphasis on certain relevant values, or perhaps because they find different arguments convincing. A particularly interesting subset, however, is constituted by moral *dilemmas* for here it is impossible for a genetics professional to take both sides. An example of this – touched upon briefly in Chapter 2 – would be where a genetic test on one patient is also at the same time a genetic test on one or more of their relatives. The situations I have in mind here are cases in which what is at stake is not simply that genetic information produced by a test in one family member is *of relevance* to another family member, but where that test is *definitive*, that is, where it reveals the other person's mutation status in the same respects and to the same degree as if they had taken the test themselves.

A 33-year-old woman was seen in genetics enquiring about predictive BRCA2 testing. Her paternal grandmother and aunts have had breast cancer and a mutation was identified in one of her paternal aunts. Her father lives in another part of the country and has, according to the patient herself, not wanted to engage in discussions about testing. He does not think it relevant to him apparently even though he has been told that if he has the same mutation his risks of certain cancers are increased. The genetics team encouraged the patient to go back to her father to discuss implications for him of her being tested – because a positive test in his daughter, combined with the information about his mother and sisters would mean that he also has the mutation – but he says he does not want to know about his genes. The woman is keen to be tested to know risks and plan surveillance. In the end we did the test and this showed her and by inference her father to have the familial mutation. It is not clear if or how this was ever communicated to her father.

Such cases involve a conflict between different key aspects of 'good practice'. The conflict in this particular case is between the genetics professional's commitment to providing care and information to her patient on the one hand, and her commitment to the idea that relatives should not be tested without their consent or appropriate counselling support on the other. This has the characteristic features of a moral dilemma because the genetics professional has good reason to provide the test to the patient for whom she has a duty of care and also has good reason not to test relatives without their consent. But it is not possible to do both of these things.

The only way of avoiding the horns of the dilemma would be for the genetics professional to use her skills and experience to encourage patients to communicate with their relatives prior to testing and reach an agreed way forward – offering them help and support with this if they find it difficult – and in many, if not most cases, she will be successful in this. Sometimes, as a result of this support, people realise the implications for their relative and decide not to proceed with the test. In other cases, the opposite occurs and the relative comes to the view that the test should go ahead for the patient's benefit despite their own personal reluctance and anxiety. But this kind of resolution is not always possible. In some scenarios, such as the one above, despite the best efforts of the genetics professional, patients continue to refuse to allow communication with their relatives, or their relatives are simply unavailable, or, when contacted, refuse permission to allow the test to proceed. In such situations the dilemma persists and the genetics professional must make a judgement between providing testing in one person, which has the potential to be a test on another person without their consent, or refusing to provide an informative test, which goes against their commitment to the care of the patient in front of them.

In practice, in cases such as the above (where a potentially life-saving intervention is available, such as breast screening, for someone with a positive BRCA test result), the test will ultimately be offered to the patient following the making of reasonable efforts to encourage and facilitate communication between family members. But this dilemma will prove much more intractable in situations where a patient wishes to pursue the option of a genetic test because they want to know their status even though no screening or other intervention is immediately available. How should a decision be made in such a case? This is a judgement about which there are genuine and strongly felt differences of opinion between genetics professionals and these tensions can sometimes manifest themselves in differences of policy between different genetics centres or between different genetics professionals. This can be problematic where it has the potential to lead to inconsistencies in the treatment of particular patients, where members of the same family are being seen by different practitioners in different genetics units, or where patients move from one centre to another.

Sometimes, in response to the genetics professional's concerns, the patient who wants the test will offer a kind of 'deal' by promising that, if the test goes ahead, they will not disclose the results of the test to their relatives. In addition to the fact that this does not avoid the issue of confidentiality (because the tested person will come to know more about the genetic status of their relative than the relative would wish them to know), genetics professionals are not usually reassured by this offer for other reasons.

I personally find just having the person say look I just won't tell her ... [not very reassuring]. I'm not suggesting that person is going to go and deliberately try and pass the information on but I suspect that bad news will get back by one channel or another so what I try to encourage them to do is to actually talk to each other and maybe both talk to us and, I think that one should try to get them to work out some sort of arrangement which might be an agreement that they won't disclose the result but also perhaps try to put in place some kind of ongoing follow-up with the person that doesn't want to know or some means of being able to pick up the pieces if they do find out, rather than just leaving them totally unsupported. But they may not want to know about that either you know, I don't think there's any kind of foolproof solution to this kind of problem but I think what I'm seriously suggesting is that we probably ought to try a bit harder than I think we probably do. [I think we have some obligation] to look after those other people.

(ii)   Differences and disagreements between professional groups within the genetics team

Something that is apparent in many of the cases discussed throughout this book, is the fact that genetics professionals often have clinical relationships with patients and their families which endure over several years and a number of generations. This means that ethical problems, too, can have an extended and complex history involving a number of different types of health professionals. In some cases, such as the one below, a practice can start out as unproblematic but become ethically troubling as it develops over time and as different health professionals become enrolled in it.

I particularly wanted to bring up one couple that we've been involved with for a number of years which has presented us with some problems. Several years ago the couple's second child was diagnosed with [a serious recessive disorder] and since then we've been involved with them through another ten pregnancies – two of which ended as spontaneous abortion. The issue which arose for us when they came to see us about the tenth pregnancy was that this was a couple who, for various reasons which I'll come to in a minute, we became convinced were using prenatal diagnosis – which obviously in the context of the risk to the pregnancy they had a right to – for sex selection. Their decisions after testing seemed to show this. They had: one affected female pregnancy which was terminated; a normal male and two carrier males, all of which were continued; and three remaining pregnancies – two normal females, and one carrier female – all three of which were terminated. An additional difficulty surrounding this particular family was that for various reasons they were previously seen by several different consultants and several different genetic counsellors and there were also sometimes different referral mechanisms because they had moved GPs and that sort of thing. Nevertheless, when we finally got to the bottom of what was going on within this family we were all convinced that they were preferentially selecting male pregnancies and it caused an awful lot of discussion in the team in our clinical meetings. The local laboratory staff in particular were more concerned than anybody because they felt that by actually disclosing the sex they were responsible for doing something which was resulting in female pregnancies being terminated. And quite a number of the laboratory staff refused to continue to test any further pregnancies, so much so that it actually got to the point where there were only about two members of the laboratory staff that would be involved in working with this family – who were pregnant again at the time, as I say. Although it was agreed that we couldn't refuse prenatal diagnosis – this left us with a real problem. So that was one family that caused us lots of problems and continue to do so because the last pregnancy – the one I'm talking about – was only this year.

An important feature of this case, and of many cases in clinical genetics, is the way in which the care of the patient and their family requires the involvement of a number of different professional groups working together. The genetics team is a complex clustering of different professions who come together around a set of shared problems. A particularly interesting juxtaposition in the case above is between those genetics professionals involved in direct clinical care (the people who meet patients) and those who work in the laboratory setting (those who do the tests). The laboratory staff are very much part of the genetics team in all genetics centres, working together on the same cases and meeting regularly to discuss the tests being done and their progress. While there are many areas in which these two professional groups share practices and agreed values, different practices, commitments and priorities can sometimes create ethical problems. One situation in which this can happen is where there is disagreement between the lab and the clinicians about the appropriateness or otherwise of a particular investigation requiring laboratory input. This occurs most frequently in the context of prenatal testing – as in the case above.

Despite the fact that there are real differences between the views and practices of laboratory staff and clinicians in this particular case the distinctions and the similarities between the different professional groups within genetics are neither fixed nor simple. There is the potential both for change and for interaction between these normative domains. It is also important to recognise that there is rarely, if ever, complete and enduring agreement *within* such professional groupings. Views in the laboratory, for example, are (as in all other areas of genetics practice), heterogeneous. Not all laboratory staff members are willing to refuse what looks like sex selection on that basis alone. This is illustrated by the case below.

A case which is presenting particular challenges to our department concerns a couple who have a son with Duchenne muscular dystrophy. They came to the department, requested prenatal diagnosis in the next pregnancy and said that if the pregnancy was female they wanted to know whether or not the daughter was a carrier as they would only wish to continue pregnancy if it was a female known not to be a carrier. They were concerned about the marriageability of a daughter who was a carrier with Duchenne. Clearly, that already raised all sorts of problems for us, but as time went by it also became apparent that they didn't really want to just avoid having a carrier daughter – they actually didn't want to have a daughter at all. After a lot of discussion in the team we decided that whereas our normal practice with prenatal diagnosis for Duchenne muscular dystrophy is to let people know the sex of the pregnancy very quickly, the offer would be made to the family [of a] more limited provision of information: they would simply be told whether the pregnancy was affected or not. They accepted that and decided to go ahead with pre-prenatal testing on that basis. We felt this was the best way forward and decided that we would ask the people in the lab to keep the sex of the pregnancy confidential. However, the people in the laboratory had some concerns about holding information in the lab and not giving it to us because this would mean that they would know more information than was to be passed on to the patient. Nevertheless, in the end the test went ahead. However, shortly after the result came out which was that the pregnancy was not affected with Duchenne we heard that they had gone on holiday overseas and had had an ultrasound scan establishing that the pregnancy was female and had a termination. They are now back again and pregnant again. And it's been very interesting how discussions around this have continued within the department. Once again we obviously have been talking a lot about whether or not we will become involved. It is interesting that the opinion from one of the people working in the labs is that perhaps we as clinical geneticists have a problem in understanding, or are reluctant to accept just how much pressure this woman who is trying to have children is under from her husband and her in-laws. And that our attempts to try and draw some sort of boundary what we feel is morally ethically reasonable is actually failing to take account of the pressure she is under, and yet none of us as clinicians feels in anyway inclined to be drawn down the path of allowing people to choose the sex of their child simply because of preference.

In addition to illustrating the diversity of moral views in each setting and the differences between them, this case and the one above it also highlight the ways in which an ethical problem can come to have a career.[2] In the case above, for example, the problem originates in a discussion about the appropriateness of carrier testing and an assessment about the implications of 'marriageability' as grounds for making this available. It then shifts into one concerned with sex selection.[3] At this point a new practice is developed – to test but not to reveal the sex of the fetus – but this compromise is not acceptable to some of the laboratory staff. The test goes ahead nonetheless and at this point the couple

[2] A. Appadurai, 'Introduction: commodities and the politics of value', in, A. Appadurai (ed.) *The Social Life of Things: Commodities in Cultural Perspective* (Cambridge University Press, 1986), pp. 3–63.

[3] A. Kerr, S. Cunningham-Burley and A. Amos, 'Eugenics and the new genetics in Britain: examining contemporary professionals' accounts' (1998) 23 *Science, Technology and Human Values*, 2, 175–198.

take matters into their own hands. They now know (because of the test result) that the fetus is either a healthy male or it is female. They go overseas and obtain a test for sex. Finding that it is female, they terminate. But the ethical problem doesn't end there. The couple are now pregnant again and now there are different voices in the laboratory which are more sympathetic to the difficulties the woman is facing and the pressures she is under.

The interface between the clinic and the laboratory is likely to become increasingly important in the future with the growing use of new technologies such as microarrays and sequencing in clinical practice and the potential for the generation of unprecedented quantities of data of potential clinical importance either immediately or in the future. One of the ways in which the use of such technologies can lead to ethical problems in practice is through the generation of what are sometimes referred to as 'incidental findings'.

I saw a five-year-old girl with developmental delay and subtle dysmorphic features. I requested array CGH testing (which has now replaced chromosome analysis as a first-line test in our service) and this showed a large deletion of a particular chunk of chromosome. This was likely to explain her clinical signs and symptoms. The problem that arose for me was that the deletion encompassed a known tumour suppressor gene which indicated a high likelihood of adult-onset cancer. Although I'd told the parents that this test might reveal something we weren't expecting, I'd only really mentioned it in very general terms and we now had a rather specific but unexpected piece of information. We discussed it as a team and weren't sure whether to tell the parents now, when they were busy worrying about her current problems, or whether to delay it for a few years since she wouldn't need any screening until her teenage years at the earliest. In the end we did tell them because we needed to check their samples to see if either of them had the same deletion. The parents were both clear but they were devastated by the fact that not only did their daughter have a genetic problem that was causing her problems now, she was also likely to develop cancer in adulthood. I think such problems are likely to arise more often as genetic technologies become broader and cheaper and I'm not sure how to deal with this with patients and families upfront.

While the ethical issues generated by the increased use of new technologies are in many respects new because of the nature and quantity of the information produced, they are also quite familiar, resonating as they do with the ethical problems discussed in Chapters 2 and 3 about the 'burdens of knowledge' and about the implications of unexpected information in the context of the genetics professional's commitment to the care of patients and their families. This suggests that in their translation into clinical practice, new genetic and genomic technologies are inevitably going to be both transformative of and themselves transformed by the existing moral commitments and practices in clinical genetics in morally significant ways.

(iii)   Encounters with other specialties

The cases discussed earlier illustrate some of the ways in which an ethical problem can come to have a career (or many) within multi-professional genetic practice as it is identified, negotiated and 'resolved' by genetics professionals, only to emerge again in a different guise at a later date. The career of an ethical problem and the role of the relations between different norms of practice in generating, negotiating and resolving such problems can be particularly visible in situations where patients are referred to clinical genetics from other specialties.[4] Although many patients will be referred directly to clinical genetics by their GP, others will arrive from another specialty such as neurology, cardiology or paediatrics. Because these specialties often have quite different settled normative practices surrounding the use of tests to those in clinical genetics, ethical problems can sometimes be generated by the movement of patients from one specialty to the other, that is, as they come in to clinical genetics from 'outside'. One way in which this movement can be particularly problematic for genetics professionals is where a patient is referred because of concern about an inherited condition, but the test or diagnosis has not been discussed prior to the referral.

We've had a number of referrals or families or cases [which] have been bounced towards us where we haven't previously had any direct involvement with the family and ... the other clinicians are passing the buck to us to kind of, pick up all the pieces. A good example of this – we've had two examples very recently – is a case in which a urologist decided to test a young adult for possibility of Kleinfelter Syndrome which he did, and it was positive. And he hadn't told the patient that he was doing this test and then he simply wrote to us and said, 'Would you mind sharing this information with the patient?' ... And we've also had another case where, quite recently, where ... a neurologist sent off some bloods as part of a research project for pre-senile dementia – sent off to the dementia research group – and eventually they found a mutation and then a pre-senile gene and we – in the genetics team – were only then asked to approach this family and pick up the pieces and deal with it; and yet we'd had absolutely no involvement and the neurologists felt out of their depth and yet we haven't said 'no' simply because we could probably handle it better.

The difficulty for the genetics professional here is that through no fault of her own she has been put in a position in which she is unable to pursue

---

[4] D. Vaughan, 'The dark side of organizations: mistake, misconduct, and disaster' (1999) 25 *Annual Review of Sociology*, 271–305.

what she considers to be good practice. The test has been done and this means that there is no longer scope for pre-test counselling or for discussion with the patient about how the communication of the result and its follow-up are to be managed. The issues at stake here arise from specialisation, and from a continuing interdependence between specialties.[5] The first of these is that clinicians in other specialties appear, from the clinical geneticist's point of view, to be carrying out or ordering genetic tests without thinking seriously about or planning for the consequences of a positive test result. They don't appreciate the difficulties that arise in the process of giving the result and addressing the issues it raises. As a consequence, when the patient arrives the genetics professional does not know what they have been told or what they are expecting. Such cases are not particularly uncommon.

[Actually] this issue of psychiatrists requesting confirmatory diagnostic tests on people who don't actually have anything other than very non-specific or allegedly behavioural features is one of the biggest problem areas that we face. We have seen problems arising from that sort of request on several occasions. I think probably in that it's professionals other than geneticists who are requesting these tests without really being fully aware of the issues involved. For example, neurology putting through tests for HD to exclude the diagnosis without really thinking what they will do if the test confirms it. Other examples include speculative testing for Prader-Willi, Fragile X.

In some cases, secondly, it is not that the health professional in the other specialty has not thought about the implications of the test but simply that following a planned test they have identified a 'counselling issue' and have referred the patient to clinical genetics because they think that this is the genetics professional's area of expertise. They don't see the connection between counselling prior to a test and what is to happen after the test.

[T]here is an assumption made by other colleagues in the medical specialties that the counsellors are very well equipped to simply pass on the information that shouldn't be a problem so if you've got the results what's the problem, you can give them to whoever comes to ask … [There is a need to raise] awareness amongst [psychiatrists and neurologists] and other specialties who probably don't realise how problematic it is.

The difficulty for the genetics professional in such cases is that, for them, what counts as good practice after a test ought to be based on the outcome of discussion prior to testing. And here again, as in previous chapters, it is important to notice that it is *because* of their practice – the

---

[5] *Ibid.*, p. 272.

practice of pre-test discussions and its relationship with post-test practice in combination with the referrals of other specialties – that the problem is created, rather than problems emerging *in the course of* their practice. Here they are faced with the problem of discussing and counselling genetic information with patients after the fact. This is difficult in all cases but is inevitably particularly so when the test result has implications for other family members or where it raises issues about relatedness.

Couple had a fetus they chose to terminate because of poor prognosis – autosomal recessive condition. They declined a post mortem so a diagnosis was not confirmed. Obstetricians arranged genetic tests on parents and fetus for a condition they were considering as a possibility. The results showed non-paternity and a copy was sent to clinical genetics (not to the parents).

From the genetics professional's perspective, other health professionals often don't seem to pay sufficient attention to such possibilities because their primary focus is the medical care of the patient. These differences have the potential to lead to important failures of communication across professional boundaries.[6]

Just as ethical problems can be generated when a patient moves from other specialties into genetics, so too can they be generated by movement in the other direction. There are a number of different ways in which genetics professionals can, for example, be dependent upon other health professionals in their attempts to maintain good working relationships with patients and families as part of their care for the *patient in the families*. Such relationships can be particularly important where the care of the patient and the family with an inherited disorder involves caring for several generations of the family over many years, particularly in the context of an inherited condition for which screening or surveillance is available. Other health professionals, importantly GPs, can play a key role in helping genetics professionals to work well with families and in many cases this aspect of multi-professional practice is effective. However, the dependence of good practice in the care of patients and families in clinical genetics upon collaboration between different professional groups can sometimes cause ethical problems. One example of this is where the genetics professional's familial practice comes into conflict with the general practitioner's commitment to acting as advocate for the individual patient.

---

[6] M. Dixon-Woods, 'Why is patient safety so hard? A selective review of ethnographic studies' (2010) 15 (Suppl. 1) *Journal of Health Services Research and Policy*, 11–16.

A pregnant woman whose husband had a strong family history of HNPCC requested a prenatal predictive test. Her husband died of cancer at thirty-eight. She says that she will terminate an affected pregnancy. The prenatal test turned out to be negative. She then reveals that she would not have terminated an affected pregnancy after all. She now says that what she wants is to know her children's HNPCC status and requests testing of her other children (without their knowledge). The woman has two other children aged six and ten. The consensus in the genetics team is that this should not happen. There is no screening available for HNPCC until one's twenties. It was decided that the best way forward was to talk to GP, work to develop and keep a good relationship with the woman and family and develop a 'road map' so that even if you don't test now it is clear to her that you are moving towards a test at some point and are on her side. Be honest and open about concerns. However, the woman's GP also wants her children to have the test immediately. He argues that the woman now already knows the result for one child (her pregnancy) and why shouldn't she be allowed to know about the others?

For the geneticist, it is very important in this case and others like it to maintain an ongoing effective relationship with the patient. Bowel screening or surveillance is going to be available for her children when they reach their early twenties and it is going to be important to ensure that they are aware of this and are able to gain easy access to it. The genetics professional would normally deal with such situations by making it clear to the woman that although they wouldn't recommend a test on a child for an adult onset condition – because no medical intervention is available at such a young age – a test would be available at some point in the future, i.e. that the conversation can continue.[7] The aim would be to strike an appropriate balance between, on the one hand, preserving future choices – the potential for the child to be involved in decision-making as an adult at the time when screening would be appropriate – and the maintenance, on the other, of an effective ongoing clinical relationship with the mother. The problem here is that the woman wants the test now and while this could usually be managed with her through negotiation and discussion, in this particular case such negotiation is made difficult because the woman is strongly supported in her request for childhood testing by the general practitioner. The genetics professional finds this frustrating because she feels that if the GP was more understanding of the issues, and of the implications of childhood testing, it would be possible to maintain a good relationship with the woman and also to provide the test when appropriate. The approach taken by the general practitioner has created a tension between the

---

[7] M. Parker, 'Genetic testing in children and young people' (2009) 9 *Familial Cancer*, 1, 15–18.

genetics professional's two goals of maintaining a good relationship and not testing children for adult-onset conditions.

In some situations genetics professionals can be even more profoundly dependent upon health professionals from other specialties. Examples include situations in which genetics professionals are involved in the care of patients they have never met and in which all care is mediated through other professionals.

This is the case of a fifty-year-old woman from a family with HNPCC in which a mutation was identified and cascade screening initiated. Through this a seventy-year-old man was identified. He has had cancer and has the mutation. He informed us about his fifty-year-old daughter who has a learning disability and lives in a residential home. We wanted to offer her testing [to see whether bowel screening was necessary] but the staff said that it would be distressing for her to be seen by someone she didn't know. In the end an agreement was reached that her GP would do it and a blood test showed her to be a gene carrier. She has never met a genetics professional. After the test, the question of arranging screening, i.e. colonoscopies, arose. She needs regular screening every two years but there was concern that she [might] not be able to keep appointments without her carers being 'on side'. This is bound to be a very distressing event for her. She has a good relationship with her carers. The lifetime risks of HNPCC in this patient are high; approximately 60 per cent of carrier women will develop bowel cancer and approximately 50 per cent will develop endometrial cancer. But genetics have never met her. All information is from GPs. The current proposal is a hysterectomy but she may never develop a cancer of the endometrium.

The concern in this case for the genetics professional has similarities with those discussed in the previous section. In this case, while there was always the possibility of a positive test result which would require screening or other intervention, the implications of this do not appear to have been thought through well or discussed with the patient by the general practitioner or the residential care worker. The problem for the genetics professional arises out of a sense of being complicit in the decision-making and in the care of this patient while at the same time being peripheral to it. The residential staff believed that contact with a health professional other than the GP would be distressing. The genetics professional accepted this, but now there is going to have to be a much more distressing interaction and the genetics professional feels that she should probably have been involved in the management of the case at an earlier stage, notwithstanding the additional distress this might have caused the patient.

The cases discussed thus far in this section have been ones in which ethical issues are created by relatively subtle differences in professional norms between the practice domains. There are some situations, however, in which other professionals are encountered by genetics professionals more explicitly as obstacles to good practice. One example of this is where genetics professionals are dependent upon other professionals for information or samples essential to the care of their patient.

A 35-year-old man was referred to us for assessment of his family history of bowel cancer. His father and uncle had died from bowel cancer in their forties. His paternal grandmother had apparently died from womb cancer. We tried to find hospital records from the deceased affected family members and to obtain a tumour sample for antibody testing since this can give a good indication of whether the cancers are likely to have been caused by a strong inherited factor (Lynch Syndrome or HNPCC). We could only find details of the paternal uncle, since he had died most recently. We wrote to the histopathology department to ask whether they would send us the hospital records and a tumour sample for testing, for the benefit of our patient. However, they wrote back that without consent from the deceased's next of kin, this would not be allowed. We had had no contact with the deceased's wife so it seemed inappropriate to ask her. We wrote back saying that the tests would help determine medical management of our patient and that as a second degree relative we believed that he could consent to access. The histopathologist refused to release the information and the sample because he thought that it would be breaking confidentiality.

In this case, the genetics professional believes that the information and sample she is requesting should be available for the care of family members. For the histopathologist who holds the sample and records of the deceased patient, however, this is personal information, part of the patient's confidential medical record, which can only be shared with the consent of the patient's next of kin.[8]

(iv) Different hats – the relationships between research and clinical practice

Previous sections have explored ethical issues created when genetics professionals and their patients encounter professionals working in different and sometimes conflicting communities of practice. The situations discussed have been ones in which patients move from one professional domain to another or where the collaboration of health professionals working in different normative domains leads to ethical problems. The relationship between competing practices can also create ethical problems in situations in which a single genetics professional wears two professional 'hats'. In this section I take one very common example of this – the interaction between research and clinical practice

---

[8] M. Parker and A. Lucassen, 'Genetic information: a joint account?' (2004) 329 *British Medical Journal*, 165–167.

in genetics – and explore how, in situations where clinicians are also researchers, these two domains of practice interact and overlap creating ethical problems for genetics professionals.[9]

The effective day-to-day care of patients and families in clinical genetics is closely interwoven with research practice. Here is one account of this, told from the perspective of someone who is both a researcher in genetics and also themselves a clinical geneticist.

A clinical geneticist telephoned a medically qualified researcher to discuss a patient with an unusual combination of clinical features. The patient presented a puzzle for diagnosis and for counselling about the genetic risk. Two months later, the clinician sent the researcher DNA from the patient, together with clinical photographs and copies of clinical letters. No mutation hotspots were found in relevant genes, and the sample was added to a 'research panel'. The clinician made further contact two years later, asking whether there were any positive results (the reply was negative) and providing some further clinical information. Eventually, a further year and a half later and after tests of thirteen genes had given negative results, the researcher contacted the clinician to say that a potentially pathogenic change in the DNA had been identified. The clinician was asked to obtain samples from the unaffected parents. The mutation was not present in either parent, establishing that the change had arisen de novo in the patient and was the cause of the clinical problem. Hence, three and a half years after the initial contact, the researcher had established unequivocally the correct diagnosis, mechanism of inheritance, and appropriate molecular test for the patient's condition. Should this be considered research or clinical investigation?[10]

This account shows how a patient's career can involve a movement, a to-ing and fro-ing, between the domains of research and clinical practice. For the researcher and the clinician the boundary between the two domains is not easy to draw or maintain.[11] In fact, for many clinician-researchers – as in the quotation above and those below – the porosity of this boundary is essential to good practice in both domains.

As a clinician-researcher I find it impossible to maintain and see this clear distinction between practice and research … This is unrealistic where you are looking at genes that are related to the search for a clinical solution. What is a clinical test, what is research?

I'm a geneticist conducting research into the causes of cranio-facial malformations in children. So I see the children and their parents in the clinic

[9] N. Hallowell, S. Cooke, G. Crawford, M. Parker and A. Lucassen, 'Defining research and clinical care: health care professionals' and researchers' understanding of cancer genetics activities' (2009) 35 *Journal of Medical Ethics*, 113–119.

[10] M. Parker, R. Ashcroft, A. Wilkie and A. Kent, 'Ethical review of research into rare genetic disorders' (2004) 329 *British Medical Journal*, 288–289.

[11] Hallowell *et al.*, 'Defining research and clinical care'.

and also run the lab that tries to find the causes of the malformations. I find it impossible to find this, kind of, clear-cut distinction between when I'm doing diagnosis and when I'm doing research because the two just, sort of, merge into one.

Though it is clearly of great importance for both research and good clinical practice, the close relationship between these two domains can nevertheless sometimes generate practical ethical problems for research-clinicians because of the juxtaposition of the different norms informing these two communities of practice.[12] An increasingly common example of this tension is where research generates findings which are, in addition to their relevance to research, also – incidentally – of clinical relevance to an individual patient or their family. In such situations, the two hats of the clinician-researcher bring with them a real sense of ethical tension.[13]

I work in cancer genetics where there's great overlap between the systems of screening. We have some forms of screening which are a part of the national screening programmes and we have other forms of screening which are part of a research study. For example, we have the Magnetic Resonance Imaging (MRI) study, which also offers mammograms as part of the study. I find this overlap quite a dilemma. As a nurse I feel very much in the front line in dealing with these families, because we do have a lot of contact. We don't just see them once. We see them again and again. I spend a lot of time with them. Recently, a woman from a family I know well joined the MRI study. She was only thirty-six but they picked up a malignancy in her breast. [Not knowing about the finding], she rang me because she knows me so well. And she said, 'oh they would tell me if they found anything, wouldn't they?' Well I knew that they'd already found something but I didn't feel that I could tell her because it had been agreed by the consultant looking after her that it wasn't appropriate for us to tell her that [research] information because it needed clinical confirmation first. Radiologist didn't tell her either. The next step was for her to have a mammogram. And the consultant geneticist wrote to the doctor doing the mammogram saying they've detected a malignancy on MRI so you need to see her quickly. So, there was something in her notes which meant that everybody knew about it except the patient, and I felt really uncomfortable with this. When she had her mammogram it wasn't detected on mammogram but they knew it was there and so they did an extra scan and confirmed it. They told the patient she'd got a malignancy and confirmed it by histology. My question is really: it's all very well in these studies when everything goes according to the plan and people are just reassured and sent on their way but if something is picked up, whose responsibility is it, you know? We are the geneticists of the

[12] N. Hallowell, S. Cooke, G. Crawford, A. Lucassen and M. Parker, 'Distinguishing research from clinical care in cancer genetics: theoretical justifications and practical strategies' (2009) 68 *Social Science and Medicine*, 2010–2017.
[13] *Ibid.*

genetic department, we enter them into these studies, we counsel them, we get them to sign the consent forms and we move them through this system. I just wondered really, you know, what that means in terms of our clinical responsibilities?

The problem for the genetics professional here is that although, in her role as a research nurse, she is required to enter patients for screening as part of a research project, she also sees them in her clinical role as a nurse and feels a sense of clinical responsibility, a duty of care, towards them. And this can lead to problems where there is a possibility that research findings will have clinical relevance. The situation in the case above is complicated because it involves a range of different types of screening, some of which are part of a national screening programme and some of which are part of a research study, each of which brings with it different norms of practice and different duties of care. Inevitably, as someone working with two hats on, these duties of care bleed into one another in ways which can create a set of difficult and sometimes irresolvable moral problems for the nurse.

Lab-based researchers too can sometimes feel unsure about what the right thing is to do with information generated through research which has some, even if uncertain, relevance to the care of patients. While the screening or testing provided through the clinical route, e.g. the National Screening Programme, is subject to quality controls and is founded upon an established evidence base (neither of which is true in the context of research), research can nevertheless sometimes have, or appear to have, implications for patients. At what point should research findings be used to guide clinical practice and who should decide?

An issue which has come up for us, is the whole question about when research becomes practice and vice versa, and when research is research in one place and practice in somewhere else. One example is Haemochromatosis. The issue here is that although there is an identified gene and there is a fair bit known about it so you can do a gene test, it's almost a susceptibility gene rather than a Mendelian disorder gene and there's still lots to be found about it, so people want to do research. The question this raises is, if you have a disorder where you know about the gene and you know that it causes the disease and the disease is preventable with appropriate measures, can you do research which doesn't involve disclosure of the result? There might be reasons to do this in some cases because if you had to disclose the results you would need to provide lots of counselling. That would be very expensive and there might be cases where if you had to fund that you couldn't do the research at all. So the ethical dilemma there is that in order to do the research, the only way you can do is if you do it unethically. But on the other hand unless you do the research you will never know, you'll never know whether the practice that you're pursuing, is actually valid or not. So there's a conflict between the value to society as against the value to the individual patient, which is difficult to resolve. Although I mentioned Haemochromatosis, that applies to lots of situations, especially where the tests which are possibly of some value to the person but maybe not of proven value. So it's just exactly at that grey interface where you're finding out about the gene and its consequences but you don't really know enough about the consequences to be able to say to someone definitely that if you have this gene your risk is x per cent having some complication in the future.

Questions about the relationship between research findings and clinical practice are becoming increasingly pressing as research and clinical practice are brought together in new ways – often in the work of a particular individual – through the use of new technologies such as microarrays and sequencing and leading to the generation of unprecedented quantities of data which may be clinically significant either immediately or at some point in the future as the understanding of such data and their implications increases.

I am involved in a project using arrays and sequencing to identify genomic features – structural rearrangements – involved in rare undiagnosed developmental disorders in order to increase our understanding of the mechanisms underlying these disorders and to develop clinical tools for better diagnosis. The project involves collecting samples from 12,000 children with undiagnosed developmental disorders and their parents – so, 36,000 samples overall. One of the things we have been struggling with a lot as the project has progressed is how to deal with data about incidental findings. The focus of the research is on the identification of changes in the genome related to the developmental disorder, but – given the numbers of samples being collected – genome-wide approaches such as those used in this project will inevitably reveal changes in the genome in a number of cases which are unrelated to the developmental disorder but are clinically relevant (for the parents, for the patient, and potentially for other siblings) such as for example, changes in genes predisposing people to cancers. The struggle we in the team have as a group of health professionals and researchers is about the extent to which we have a duty of care to feed this information back to participants and/or their clinicians (the patients are being recruited though a large number of geographically dispersed clinical genetics units). One way forward would be to decide not to feedback anything which is unrelated to the developmental disorder but this doesn't address those cases in which the features of the genome responsible for the developmental disorder turn out to be close to the incidental finding, for example where the deletion responsible for the developmental disorder overlaps with a cancer predisposing gene.

There is currently a great deal of debate about this problem and about how the data produced through the use of such technologies should be managed. It is likely that one of the most interesting implications of these developments is going to be the way in which it becomes increasingly difficult to separate out the obligations of clinicians from those of researchers. If, for example, as seems likely, a position is ultimately adopted that a limited range of – clinically significant – information will be fed back from researchers to clinicians, agreement about what in any particular context is to constitute reportable information is going to call for discussion between research groups and clinicians, and the management and feeding back of such data to clinical teams will to a large extent be carried out by researchers who are not clinically trained. This suggests that researchers may increasingly come to be seen to be playing important roles in the *clinical* process with the potential for this to generate new professional obligations and new ethical problems for them as researchers.

Even if it were to be agreed that there are some situations in which research *findings* should not influence patient care, ethical issues can also – as exemplified in the case below – be generated by the existence of material resources such as blood or tissue samples produced and stored for research purposes with the potential for clinical use.

This case concerns a family known to have a history of breast cancer. One member of the family recently died of lymphoma and near to her death consented to the use of a blood sample for a research project. It is assumed that her lymphoma was part of the syndrome related to the family history. This being the case, is it acceptable to use the sample for the benefit of the deceased patient's relatives if this will make it possible to carry out predictive genetic tests on them? The concern here is that consent was given for the use of the sample in research, not in clinical practice. A further question concerned whether it made a difference to the decision if the sample was part of her health record, rather than part of a research project.

One very practical ethical concern genetics professionals can have about the blurring of the boundary between research and clinical practice is where patients who are research participants may be confused about whether or not they are undergoing treatment.[14]

This concerned a research study that explored the familial aspects of upper GI cancer. The study was to be carried out within the context of providing clinical service and offering mutation testing. Often when a patient is seen they are already terminally ill. The plan is for a researcher-clinician to take the samples. We have had discussions about whether this is an acceptable time to take consent. Partly it is because of a concern about the competence of patients but also we are worried about the therapeutic misconception, i.e. that they might mistake the research for treatment. Raises difficult issues about the relationship between clinical practice and research.

---

[14] *Ibid.*; P.S. Appelbaum and L.H. Roth, 'The therapeutic misconception: informed consent in psychiatric research' (1982) 5 *International Journal of Law and Psychiatry*, 319–329.

The worry about the 'therapeutic misconception' here is that if a research participant mistakenly believes themselves to be being offered a clinically indicated intervention, their consent to the research may be invalid both in relation to the question of whether it is adequately informed and also in relation to its voluntariness – because the decision to participate in research may be influenced by the mistaken belief that the intervention offers a proven therapeutic benefit and/or that the person inviting them to undergo the intervention is acting in her capacity as their doctor.

The cases discussed in this section have explored the ethical difficulties generated for genetics professionals by the close relationship between clinical practice and research in their day-to-day practice and by the widely held view that it is important to maintain a clear boundary between these two normative domains. The boundaries between research and clinical practice are not only maintained by genetics professionals as clinician-researchers, but are also sometimes required by regulatory structures.[15] These forms of regulation can also have important ethical implications both for clinical practice and the care of patients and for research.

And the other example that I had was of a child with a rare tumour who happened to have a balanced translocation where the balanced translocation went through an area that by linkage had been shown to be responsible for a cancer syndrome. So I then asked for the family's consent and sent tumour blocks from this child to somebody researching into this condition. But then, despite the fact that the family had given their consent, the histopathologist who held the tumour blocks said that she wouldn't release the tumour blocks before she saw the [research ethics committee] approval and of course this wasn't a study that had been specifically designed for patients but was a research study looking at a disease locus so there was no, there was no ethical approval. So again, I thought that highlighted the sort of tension between research and clinical because for us often I think that feels like sort of clinical duty to be finding people who are interested in research in particular genetic condition.

(v)   The world 'outside' clinical genetics

This chapter began with an exploration of the ways in which the differences between individual genetics professionals about particular cases and between the practices of different professional groups within genetics – such as laboratory staff and clinicians – can create ethical problems. It went on to look at the ways in which ethical difficulties can also be created by the differences between the practices of genetics

---

[15] Hallowell *et al.*, 'Distinguishing research from clinical care'.

professionals and those of health professionals outside of clinical genetics with whom they interact. This was followed by an investigation of the ethical problems created by situations in which individual genetics professionals inhabit multiple normative domains of professional practice simultaneously, taking the overlap between research and clinical practice as an example.

The maintenance of boundaries between domains of professional practice and the practices 'outside' are inevitably only ever partially successful.[16] Patient careers, and hence the careers of ethical problems, frequently loop outside of the domain of the genetics professional and sometimes even outside of the health professions altogether in ways that have the potential to generate – or perhaps on occasion to erase – ethical problems. The possibility of patients and their families slipping off-stage and gaining access to services or advice elsewhere offers important challenges to what might otherwise be unproblematic norms of day-to-day practice. In some cases, this is because the genetics professional – and perhaps the patient – is aware of different approaches in other areas of medical practice. In the cases discussed in Chapter 4, for example, in which genetics professionals were concerned about patients who requested access to prenatal testing for 'minor conditions', it became apparent that the criteria for access to termination of pregnancy in clinical genetics are different to those applied elsewhere – for example in general practice. Whatever the merits or otherwise of managing access to prenatal testing and termination of pregnancy in particular ways in the context of clinical genetics, such practices create ethical difficulties (and also perhaps ethical solutions) in situations where patients are able to go to another medical professional and gain access to the service being refused by genetics professionals. What this illustrates is that the power of genetics professionals to define and manage what is to count as unproblematic (or problematic) practice – even within the context of a national health service – will not always be completely in their own hands and this itself has the potential to create problems around the important moral commitments to multi-professional practice.

In addition to the ways in which patient careers, and the careers of ethical problems, can sometimes move between different professional domains in a particular setting, the increasing ease with which people, information and technologies move internationally also means that there

[16] T.F. Gieryn, 'Boundary-work and the demarcation of science from non-science: strains and interests in professional ideologies of scientists' (1983) 48 *American Sociological Review*, 6, 781–795; A. Kerr, S. Cunningham-Burley and A. Amos, 'The new genetics: professionals' discursive boundaries' (1997) 45 *The Sociological Review*, 2, 279–303.

is the potential for an international circulation of patients and information relating to genetics. This 'global cultural flow' can have important ethical implications for day-to-day practice and can place limits upon the extent to which genetics professionals can manage the legitimate uses and implications of their practice.[17] This potential is illustrated by the second sex-selection case discussed earlier in this chapter. In this case, a pregnant woman who already has a son with Duchenne muscular dystrophy requested prenatal testing for the condition and asked to be informed of the carrier status of the pregnancy should it turn out to be female. Because of concerns that the woman might be considering terminating all female pregnancies, and to avoid being complicit in sex selection, the genetics team decided to provide the couple only with information about whether the pregnancy was affected or not, and not about the sex of the fetus. This was acceptable to the couple. The genetics professionals later learned that, having been informed that the pregnancy was not affected, the couple went overseas and, on the basis of an ultrasound which established that the pregnancy was female, had a termination. This is a good illustration of how an attempt to maintain normative practice (in this case to avoid sex selection) fails because patients and families have access to resources, networks and connections which enable them to achieve what it is that they want.

Inevitably, the Internet too can offer a way in which the world 'outside' can become relevant to the effectiveness and development of practices in clinical genetics. In the case below, a genetics professional wonders whether she should set aside her worries about the testing of children in order to ensure that the woman, who may become aware of the availability of prenatal testing on the Internet and pursue it, has access to appropriate counselling.

[T]he thing is that in my mind, if this woman is desperate enough for this information, she will get it one way or another, there will always be a route for her, not necessarily through the clinical genetic service but I'm sure if you looked hard enough on the Internet you would find some[one] you know that would be willing to do a test and so I just think it's interesting to ponder whether it's sometimes better to go down the route with her coming in and receiving counselling having the amnio, even if she doesn't undergo a termination afterwards as opposed to a theoretical alternative her going down some other route and not having counselling and not sort of ensuring she gets all the best information she can.

These cases illustrate some of the ways in which the genetics professional's moral world is open and subject to unpredictable disruption by

---

[17] A. Appadurai, *Modernity at Large* (Minneapolis: University of Minnesota Press, 1996), pp. 27–47.

the world outside of both the professional domain of the genetics professional and even of the health professions more broadly.

Conclusion

Like those in previous chapters, the cases discussed above were presented at the Genethics Club by genetics professionals as ethical problems. What this suggests is that, in addition to the features of the moral world of the genetics professional discussed in Chapters 2, 3 and 4 – those arising out of the genetics professional's commitments to caring for the patient in 'the families'; their ability to see connections and recognise differences between the family as biology and the family as culture; and the complexities of their commitment to patient-centred care – ethical problems can also be generated by the coming together in 'multi-professional practice' of the normative practices of different genetics professionals, different communities of practice within genetics and in other specialties, and situations in which genetics professionals wear different hats such as those of researcher and clinician.

The chapter began with an investigation of situations in which there are differences within the context of the multi-professional genetics team itself, first by considering situations in which there are differences between individual genetics professionals when confronted by a moral dilemma and, second, through discussion of the example of the different views of laboratory staff and clinical geneticists about the generation of information relevant to the patient's family. It then examined how similar tensions can be generated by situations in which patients move from one professional domain into another, for example where patients are referred into clinical genetics from other clinical settings such as neurology with different approaches to what constitutes good practice in the clinical use of genetics. The chapter then went on to explore how conflicts can arise in situations where genetics professionals are dependent upon other professional groups for information or tests for what they consider to be the good care of their patients, e.g. where different professional groups have approaches to consent which make it difficult to obtain information about test results in family members. Following this, I discussed those situations in which, rather than patients moving between professional domains, it is the individual genetics professional herself who wears two hats, e.g. that of the clinician and the researcher, and where each of these roles brings with it conflicting approaches to the commitments underpinning good practice. The chapter concluded with an exploration of how the commitments of everyday practice of genetics professionals can create ethical difficulties when placed in a global context. The porosity of domains of normative practice, their endurance and their interactions are of real significance for the moral dimensions of genetics practice.

6   Moral craft

'Craftsmanship' may suggest a way of life that waned with the advent of industrial society – but this is misleading. Craftsmanship names an enduring, basic human impulse, the desire to do a job well for its own sake. Craftsmanship cuts a far wider swath than skilled manual labor; it serves the computer programmer, the doctor, and the artist; parenting improves when it is practiced as a skilled craft, as does citizenship. In all these domains, craftsmanship focuses on objective standards, on the thing in itself. Social and economic conditions, however, often stand in the way of the craftsman's discipline and commitment: schools may fail to provide the tools to do good work, and workplaces may not truly value the aspiration for quality. And though craftsmanship can reward an individual with a sense of pride in work, this reward is not simple. The craftsman often faces conflicting objective standards of excellence; the desire to do something well for its own sake can be impaired by competitive pressure, by frustration, or by obsession.[1]

When the Genethics Club was established in 2001, it was intended as a one-off workshop bringing together genetics professionals, policy-makers and bioethicists to discuss the ethical issues arising in clinical genetics.[2] When organising this meeting we had no expectation that it would lead to what has in fact followed: the Genethics Club has, at the time of writing, become a kind of institution. It has met thirty times in different places around the country, has been attended by very large numbers of genetics professionals and has been formally adopted as a special interest group of the British Society for Human Genetics.[3] Those who have attended have included nurses, counsellors, clinical geneticists, NHS laboratory staff, and health professionals from a wide

---

[1] R. Sennett, *The Craftsman* (London: Penguin, 2008), p. 9.
[2] The Genethics Club is currently organised by Anneke Lucassen, Angus Clarke, Tara Clancy and Mike Parker. See Chapter 1 for more details about its formation and development.
[3] Information about the British Society for Human Genetics can be found at www.bshg.org.uk.

range of other specialties involving the clinical use of genetics. A small core group of genetics professionals have attended virtually all of the meetings. The majority have attended several. Attendance at individual meetings has ranged from twenty to sixty-five, with an average attendance of something like thirty. In total, several hundred different people have attended. It is striking that attendance at Genethics has been confined neither to one or two centres nor to a small number of ethics enthusiasts, but has had a broad appeal.

Over time the format of the meetings has evolved into one structured around cases presented by genetics professionals, followed by open discussion – to some extent this follows the format established by the Dysmorphology Club, which is familiar to genetics professionals. The number of cases to be presented at a particular meeting is established as attendees introduce themselves at the beginning of the day and the time available divided up accordingly. Other than this, discussion at the meetings tends to be free-flowing. Approximately 250 cases have been formally presented overall and the discussion following these presentations has prompted the wide-ranging exploration of many more cases, partial cases and issues.

Other than for the first meeting in 2001, the Genethics Club has received no external funding. The people who attend pay a small fee (£10 or £15 per meeting) to cover the cost of room hire and lunch, and they pay their own travel expenses. Some of them pay this from their own pocket, others are able to claim it back from their units' training budgets. Given this, it is interesting to reflect upon why it is that the Genethics Club has been so popular with genetics professionals. Why is it that they come to the Genethics Club in such numbers, and at their own expense? What do they get out of it? Why, moreover, do their line-managers and clinical leads support them in this, and allow them to take time out of work to attend? Given the busy working lives of health professionals, and the pressure of the demands on the units in which they work, this is not easy to understand.

Perhaps unsurprisingly, in many instances attendance at the Genethics Club has been initially prompted by a particularly difficult case. This is reflected in the fact that the 'cases' genetics professionals bring along to the Genethics Club tend to be presented as ethical problems they have encountered in the care of their patients and their families. So, one reason why genetics professionals attend Genethics Club is that they have met with a problem and would like to discuss this with colleagues.

While this explanation seems right for many first-time attendees, it does not really account for why it is that so many genetics professionals from such diverse backgrounds continue to attend, coming back again and again even when they have no case to present or discuss. Why do they do this? On reflection, it seems to me that a key motivation for continued or repeat attendance for many seems to be something like a commitment to 'good practice'.[4] The majority of those who participate in the Genethics Club appear to share a desire to do their job well for its own sake and recognise that this requires not only good practice with regard to the clinical or medical aspects of their day-to-day work but also a commitment to what might perhaps be thought of as the 'moral craft' of genetics. It is this which appears to motivate them to take seriously the problems they encounter in their own practice and which informs their willingness and interest in learning about and discussing the problems encountered by others. In this respect, the genetics professionals who attend exhibit the kinds of commitments identified by Richard Sennett with 'craftsmanship' in the quotation with which this chapter began.

Drawing upon the discussion in previous chapters, I want now to explore the relationships between 'problems' and 'solutions' in the context of the genetics professional's commitment to do a job well for its own sake, and the roles they play in the Genethics Club and in genetics practice more widely.

Moral practices

Genetics is frequently identified in the media and by policy-makers and academics working in bioethics as a form of contemporary life permeated by profoundly challenging ethical and social 'issues'. But for genetics professionals themselves, such challenges are relatively infrequent and are experienced as contrasting with a broad background of day-to-day practice which is relatively stable and unproblematic. Clinical genetics has been practised as a profession since the 1940s[5] – becoming well established in the 1960s – long before the development of genetic testing and, over this time, clinical geneticists, nurses and genetic counsellors have developed widely accepted and effective models of good practice.[6] Patients are seen, histories are taken, screening is offered, treatments are given and relatives are informed as genetics professionals come to care for successive generations and multiple branches of families. It is perhaps paradoxical that one of the things that the development of the

---

[4] I draw here upon my experience of participation in the Genethics Club and in clinical genetics more broadly – as described in Chapter 1.

[5] P. Harper, *A Short History of Medical Genetics* (Oxford University Press, 2008), pp. 271–312.

[6] *Ibid.*

Genethics Club and the presentation of cases there as 'problematic' has served to highlight most powerfully is the extent to which ethical problems emerge against and need to be understood in the context of a rich background of complex but largely agreed day-to-day practice. Most of the time genetics professionals do not worry about moral problems or see their practices as problematic. They simply get on with their job.

To say that practice in genetics tends not to be characterised on a daily basis by ethical conflict, controversy and ambiguity, or by a constant requirement for reflection and critique, is not to say that it is not moral. The fact that practices can be deeply moral even when not obviously problematic is sometimes overlooked by those who identify ethics with conflict, disagreement or uncertainty – those who think in terms of ethical 'issues'. But one of the striking things about the discussion of cases in the earlier chapters of this book is the way that the world of the genetics professional emerges as richly moral even when not characterised by what might conventionally be seen as ethical issues. In their day-to-day practice, genetics professionals make not only scientific or clinical judgements about, for example, the quality of the evidence for one intervention in comparison with another, or about the interpretation of a particular dysmorphology and its implications for future health, but also value judgements. Such judgements are often explicit. An example of this would be situations in which genetics professionals made it clear that they considered prenatal testing and termination of pregnancy to be inappropriate for 'minor' conditions (see Chapter 4). Or, sometimes value judgements are explicitly stated in guidelines or in the law – for example when professional guidelines state that a patient's confidentiality may be breached where there is a 'risk of death or serious harm' to the patient or to a third party;[7] or the requirements for valid consent established in law. In many cases, however, value judgements are not explicit but are implicit in what seem at first glance to be 'clinical' decisions. Genetics professionals may not think of themselves as making value judgements when considering what would be in an incompetent patient's 'best interests', when deciding whether an inherited condition is sufficiently 'serious' to justify prenatal testing, or when making judgements about 'prioritising' the department's spending on genetic testing or PGD. Yet, these decisions do involve value judgements. Such judgements can also be implicit in practice in ways which do not have the characteristics of decisions at all. Indeed, perhaps the majority of value judgements are simply built into the genetics professional's day-to-day encounters with patients as smooth practices

---

[7] General Medical Council, *Confidentiality* (London: General Medical Council, 2009).

embodying implicit, unspoken values. Among other things, these might include: caring about, listening carefully to and having respect for the views, attitudes and beliefs of patients; having the courage to be honest; breaking bad news in ways that are sensitive; taking the time to do things well – not rushing; providing 'support'. The chapters in this book have also highlighted that value judgements are built into the various material practices and objects which play a key role in genetics, e.g. consent forms, pedigrees, blood samples, photographs, the ways in which files are stored and accessed. The value judgements that characterise the relatively unproblematic day-to-day moral practices of clinical genetics have an important material dimension.

The day-to-day moral practices of genetics professionals, even where relatively unproblematic, are not uniform and it is important not to over-emphasise their homogeneity. There is tremendous diversity of values and social and cultural practices both in patients and health professionals as well as between institutions, and this has been a feature of many of the cases discussed in the previous chapters. It is striking nonetheless that despite the existence of diversity there remains a wide range of relatively unproblematised practice which acts as a stable background out of which the problems discussed in this book emerge and into which solutions recede. It is apparent from these cases that the moral world of the conscientious genetics professional is informed by a number of important and largely shared moral commitments. The commitment to caring for patients and their families is, for example, shared relatively unquestioningly by all of the genetics professionals I encountered despite their diversity in other respects. It is one of the key features of the moral world of the genetics professional. This brings with it, among other things, a commitment to patient-centredness, respect for the patient's beliefs and values, respect for their wishes, and a broad approach which is sometimes described as 'non-directive'.[8] As was seen in Chapter 2, the commitment to the care of the patient's family, which is in many respects peculiar to the world of clinical genetics, arises from the fact that information about inherited disorders in the patient, or the finding that they are not at risk, almost inevitably has implications for their relatives. The process of working with the patient often generates information about other people for whom the geneticist starts to develop a sense of responsibility. Views about the nature and strength

---

[8] B. Burke and A. Kolker, 'Directiveness in prenatal genetic counselling' (1994) 22 *Women and Health*, 31–53; A. Clarke, 'The process of genetic counselling: beyond nondirectiveness', in P. Harper and A. Clarke, *Genetics, Society and Clinical Practice* (Oxford: Bios Scientific Publishing, 1997), pp. 179–200.

of these obligations vary greatly, but in general genetics professionals see themselves as having at least some responsibility to make reasonable efforts to ensure that information is shared with at-risk family members and to enable them to have access to support, information, testing and treatment or screening. This commitment manifests itself in encouragement to patients to talk to their relatives, in the writing of letters to be passed on to relatives by the patient and so on, and can involve providing care and support both to family members who are biologically related to the patient and those who are related to them in other ways, e.g. as partners or carers.

The complexities of contemporary family life inevitably mean that there is much interplay and slippage between these commitments, and their implications work out differently in the context of different patients and families and in the context of different inherited disorders. That is, these commitments, while broadly shared, require interpretation and judgement in particular cases. Such judgements will be guided by experience and rules of thumb which together make up 'good practice': listening, paying attention, being 'supportive' – waiting, allowing time to pass, writing letters to, or calling, GPs – and so on.

The moral world of the clinical geneticist is, then, characterised by broad areas of relatively stable and unproblematic practice constituted by moral commitments such as those to the patient and her family and implicit and explicit value judgements manifested in interpretive rules of thumb, material practices and so on which are themselves in practice largely shared. An interesting story could be told about how it is that such moral practices, rules of thumb and the shared values integral to good practice emerged over the course of the history of the development of clinical genetics and how they are maintained within the day-to-day practices of genetics professions and passed on from one generation of genetics professionals to the next. That is, about how genetics professionals are introduced to and come to take over the values, commitments, habits and implicit practices, traditions and views about good practice which characterise the profession of clinical genetics. It is likely that this involves both explicit and tacit processes. Some of the commitments and other moral practices informing good practice in genetics are likely to have been explicitly taught in medical school, on nursing courses or in genetic counsellor training, and reinforced in continuing professional development. Some are explicitly stated in law or in professional guidelines – for example in the General Medical Council's guidance on confidentiality[9] or in the British Society for Human Genetics

---

[9] General Medical Council, *Confidentiality* (London: General Medical Council, 2009).

guidelines on genetic testing in children.[10] Much of what counts as good practice, important values and appropriate rules of thumb is however either not amenable to being taught explicitly, or is taught much more powerfully through the 'hidden curriculum' outside of the ethics seminars – on the wards or in the 'clinical' lectures. It is also, moreover, as moral practice, likely to involve the kinds of skills, attitudes and practices which can be shown but cannot be taught or explained.[11] Just as in surgery, for example, where the surgeon's experienced judgement that what looks like a case of x – requiring immediate surgery – is in fact a case of y – which does not require surgery at all – is frequently a skill or judgement learnt through experience and close practice with experienced colleagues (rather than something explicitly taught), so this is also likely to be the case with much moral judgement. This is the way in which young doctors, nurses and counsellors come to learn the character traits and the virtues of the good genetics professional, i.e. how to relate to, how to speak to, how to listen and take seriously, how to 'care' and so on. Much of the formation of virtue and character, which is so central to good practice and the moral world of the genetics professional, is inevitably made possible by personal experience and through engagement with the experiences of others; by means, that is of taking part in a form of apprenticeship. This is because much of what is moral and what is good practice emerges from and is implicit in practice and is not the product of the application of ethical principles or frameworks *to* problems or practices. It is established through the formation of shared habits of good practice and the growth of practical wisdom.[12]

Moral work

To say that much of the practice of the genetics professional is relatively stable and unproblematic – underpinned by a rich heritage of tacit knowledge and shared approaches to good practice – is not in any sense to suggest that it is uncomplicated or that genetics professionals are not called upon to make difficult value judgements in their day-to-day work with patients and families. It is clear from the cases and discussion presented in this book that they frequently are. The complexities

---

[10] British Society for Human Genetics, *Genetic Testing of Children* (Birmingham: British Society for Human Genetics, 2010) available at www.bshg.org.uk/GTOC_2010_BSHG.pdf (accessed 1 August 2011).
[11] J. Dewey, *Human Nature and Conduct* (New York: Prometheus Books, 2002), pp. 177–178.
[12] *Ibid.*; Aristotle, *Nicomachean Ethics* (London: Penguin, 1976).

of practice and of family life mean that shared practice is only ever *relatively* stable, and commitments are always to some extent *provisional*. Clinical genetics is a challenging job and one of the most striking features of the moral world of the genetics professional as it emerges in the previous chapters is the tremendous amount of work required on a daily basis in order to carry out this job successfully, even against the background of relatively stable, unproblematic day-to-day practices and commitments.

I suggested above that the maintenance of the core and relatively widely agreed and unproblematic commitment to the care of the patient, for example, requires of genetics professionals that they work out in particular instances just what such care requires and what are the implications of their commitments to good practice in situations which are often both dynamic and complex. What exactly is required in this particular case by: caring; taking responsibility for; treating with respect and so on? How and when should bad news be broken to this patient? When is it appropriate to raise the issue of sharing information with the patient's relatives? How is it best to manage the process of discussing the implications of a possible predictive test in their children? Much of this work will be informed by rules of thumb and tacit understanding based on the clinician's experience of what has proved effective in the past and by what he or she has learnt from the experiences of colleagues. Families differ in important ways, but they also often have much in common to which the experience of the genetics professional is relevant and might usefully and appropriately be brought to bear. This means that in many cases, genetics professionals will know how to negotiate their way through these kinds of problems without having to think very hard or long about it. But this will not always be the case. Sometimes genetics professionals will worry about such problems and discuss with their colleagues how best to implement or interpret the principles and commitments of good practice in particular situations and contexts.

The genetics professional will also encounter situations in which there are tensions in practice between competing moral commitments or value judgements, e.g. between care for the patient and care for her family, or between different conceptions of good practice. In the context of particular families it is not uncommon for these commitments, because they pull in different directions, to seem to call for conflicting courses of action. This can arise in situations, such as those discussed in Chapter 2, where patients refuse to share information with their family members, for example. Here the commitment to caring for the individual patient and respecting his or her confidentiality is in practical tension with the commitment to ensuring that other family members who are at risk and who may benefit from contact with genetics professionals are informed and offered support and advice. In this kind of situation, the successful management of the tension between two commitments, and the achievement of a solution which respects both, requires a different kind of work. Experienced genetics professionals tend to be extremely good at this. In such situations the experienced geneticist will counsel the patient, supporting her and offering advice and, while remaining steadfastly patient centred, encourage her to see the importance of the sharing of information and suggest ways in which this might be possible. This is the process of negotiation, mediation, encouragement and support by means of which genetics professionals make it possible for patients to share information with family members despite their anxiety, or initial reluctance to do so.[13] This is how the genetics professional does the work required for it to be possible to meet her obligations both to the patient and to her family. And it is the effective carrying-out of this work, guided by the use of moral rules of thumb, which has enabled the commitments and practices underpinning good practice to be maintained and met.

Good practice is not merely a matter of following rules of thumb or practising according to agreed principles or commitments. Principles and commitments require interpretation in practice and the tensions between them need to be managed. Judgements need to be made. What all of this means is that the day-to-day practice of genetics is characterised by a huge amount of what might be thought of as 'moral work'[14] and it is this moral work which sustains the key ethical commitments to patients and their families as discussed in Chapter 2, to the family as biology and the family as 'culture' as discussed in Chapter 3, to patient-centredness in the context of the complexities of particular cases, ambiguity and uncertainty as discussed in Chapter 4, and to multi-professional practice in the context of resource and institutional constraints as discussed in Chapter 5. If much of everyday practice

[13] See, for example, A. Clarke, M. Richards, L. Kerzin-Storrar, J. Halliday, M.A. Young, S. Simpson, K. Featherstone, K. Forrest, A. Lucassen, P.J. Morrison, O.W.J. Quarrell, H. Stewart and collaborators, 'Genetic professionals' reports of nondisclosure of genetic risk information within families' (2005) 13 *European Journal of Human Genetics*, 556–562.

[14] T.F. Gieryn, 'Boundary-work and the demarcation of science from non-science: strains and interests in professional ideologies of scientists' (1983) 48 *American Sociological Review*, 6, 781–795.

in genetics is relatively stable and unproblematic, this is largely made possible and held together by the moral work of genetics professionals.

Ethical objects of concern

The moral work of genetics professionals is largely successful in holding the moral practices of day-to-day genetics together – in sustaining the shared commitments and their enactment in 'good practice'. Nevertheless, as the cases presented at the Genethics Club show, there are some situations in which the commitments informing good practice are brought into question and can themselves become objects of concern. And situations too, in which the moral work by which these commitments are sustained, can also come to be seen as problematic. Against a background of broad agreement, shared practices and continuing moral work, these cases are experienced by the genetics professionals who present them, and by those who come along to listen and discuss them at the Genethics Club, as a particular kind of problem calling for a particular kind of moral work – a kind of work that I will call 'ethics'.

In this book, I have mapped out four main ways in which the everyday practices of clinical genetics can create ethical problems around the moral commitments of genetics professionals. Taking as its starting point the genetics professional's commitment to the care of the patient in the family, Chapter 2 explored some of the ways in which ethical problems are created by the construction and verification of the family pedigree and the creation of the 'master pedigree' through which the 'family' is transformed into an assemblage of 'families' and the commitment to the patient in the family becomes a commitment to the 'patient in the families'. It began with an exploration of the ways in which this commitment can pull in different directions as a result of knowledge relevant to the care of individual patients to which genetics professionals have access as a result of their experience of working with several generations or branches of the patient's wider family, or as a result of their access to the contents of the family file. It then went on to examine how such knowledge can create ethical difficulties for genetics professionals because of tensions between their concern to use the knowledge to benefit the patient on the one hand and their concern to respect the family members from whom the information was obtained on the other. It concluded with an exploration of other ways in which the genetics professional's commitment to the patient and his or her family can become an ethical problem, including situations in which patients refuse to share potentially beneficial information with family members, and those in which the care of the genetics professional's own patient is dependent upon the obtaining of information from other family members or from the clinicians responsible for their care.

Building upon the account of the implications of tensions within the genetics professional's commitment to the care of the patient and his or her family developed in Chapter 2, Chapter 3 went on to illustrate the multiplicity of the family pedigree and of the genetics professional's commitment to the family through an exploration of the difficulties which arise for genetics professionals out of the differences and similarities between the family understood as biological connectedness on the one hand and as social relatedness on the other. This chapter explored how the interplay between the family understood as biology and the family understood as social relatedness has the potential to lead to the emergence of the genetics professional's commitment to 'the family' as an ethical problem. It began with an analysis of situations in which patients are willing for information about genetic risk to be shared with family members but wish to specify the limits of the family in ways which did not accord with the genetics professional's sense of the scope and relevance of the information and of their obligations – where for example, patients insist that certain relatives do not count as part of the family and should therefore not have access to familial information. It then went on to look at situations in which families were socially separated, perhaps through divorce or estrangement, and keen to resist the kinds of relatedness which the sharing of genetic information would produce. Finally, it explored the ethical difficulties created for genetics professionals in situations where a genetic test reveals the biological family structure to be different to the way it has been presented by patients or their families, e.g. through the revelation of misattributed paternity or the identification of unsuspected adoption.

Like those in previous chapters, the cases discussed in Chapter 4 were also ones in which ethical problems are created around the important moral commitments of genetics professionals by the everyday practices of clinical genetics. Taking reproductive medicine as its focus, this chapter explored some of the ways in which the emphasis on information-giving, non-directiveness and value-neutrality – and the relationships between them – can create ethical problems for the genetics professional committed to patient-centredness. It began with an investigation of situations in which patients want access to treatments or tests which conflict with what the genetics professional considers to be appropriate, e.g. situations where pregnant women want access to prenatal testing and termination of pregnancy for 'minor' conditions. It then went on to look at cases in which requests for prenatal testing were made by women who had no plans to terminate an affected pregnancy and at the tensions this generated between the concern for the reproductive choices of women on the one hand and concern about childhood testing on the other. It then investigated questions about the management of access to preimplantation genetic diagnosis in the context of high levels of demand. The chapter concluded with an examination of situations in which prenatal testing in one patient generates information of relevance to other family members. This involved returning briefly to some of the themes mapped out in Chapter 2 – and especially the family understood as multiple – to explore how they are manifested in the particular setting of reproductive medicine.

Taken together, Chapters 2, 3 and 4 examined how tensions between the commitments informing approaches to good practice in genetics can lead to the emergence of those commitments and practices as problems for genetics professionals. Building on this discussion, Chapter 5 went on to analyse the ways in which the multi-professional context of genetics practice can lead to the emergence of problems in practice because genetics professionals and the different professional groups with which they work place different emphases on these commitments and their relative importance. It began with an investigation of situations in which there were differences within the context of the multi-professional genetics team itself – an example of this was the different views of laboratory staff and clinical geneticists about the generation of information relevant to the patient's family – and then went on to look at how similar tensions can be generated by situations in which patients move from one professional domain into another. For example, where patients are referred into clinical genetics from other clinical settings such as neurology which have different approaches to what constitutes good practice in the clinical use of genetics. The chapter showed how conflicts can also arise in situations where genetics professionals are dependent upon other professional groups for information or tests for what they consider to be the good care of their patients, e.g. where different professional groups have approaches to consent which make it difficult to obtain information about test results in family members. This was followed by an exploration of situations in which, rather than patients moving between professional domains, it is the individual genetics professional him or herself who wears two hats, e.g. that of the clinician and the researcher, and where each of these roles brings with it conflicting approaches to the commitments underpinning good practice. Chapter 5 concluded with an investigation of some of the ways in which the commitments of everyday practice in genetics can come to emerge as problematic in contexts where patients and families have access to resources, networks and connections internationally which enable them to circumvent established practices.

The cases presented by genetics professionals at the Genethics Club are examples of situations in which moral work and the conditions which sustain and make moral work possible no longer reassure or convince. These are occasions on which their rules of thumb and implicit and explicit commitments no longer provide solutions to the problems encountered, but rather are seen to generate more problems, or perhaps problems of different kinds. These are not merely the kind of situations which require the genetics professional to stop, pause and think carefully about what they are doing, e.g. how should I go about telling this patient that they do in fact have a high risk of developing breast cancer, or how can I support this patient in ways which make it possible for them to discuss the risks with their family members? Genetics professionals do not come to Genethics Club for advice about this kind of problem even though they evidently call for a significant amount of moral work. The cases they bring to the Genethics Club are those in which the commitments, principles and practices underpinning 'good practice' (including moral work) are called into question and are themselves problematic. These are 'ethical' problems – occasions of moral stumbling.[15] And these are clearly very significant problems for those who take the idea of good practice and of doing their job well seriously because they render unstable the very question of what is to count as good practice.

Problem-seeking

What are the implications of the preceding discussion for ways of thinking about the roles of ethics in the day-to-day practice of genetics professionals and for understanding the relationship between moral practices and ethics?

The argument I am developing can be summarised thus far, like this. Genetics professionals have a job to do. They need to be able to care for patients and their families and to fulfil their other professional obligations without having to reflect upon or deliberate about each and every aspect of their practice. Were this necessary it would prove unsettling both for the patient and for genetics professionals themselves and good practice would be impossible. In genetics, as in any other area of life, this means that much moral practice is unreflective

---

[15] M. Mandelbaum, *Phenomenology of Moral Experience* (Baltimore: Johns Hopkins Press, 1969).

and embedded in settled practices and habits which carry the accumulated valuable experience of the past into the present.[16] Morality only makes sense in the context of some shared established practices and values. Problems such as the ones described earlier in this chapter are, however, also an unavoidable part of the day-to-day practice of the genetics professional – and these problems are frequently acute because genetics professionals have duties of care to particular patients and their families and decisions often need to be made within tight time constraints (such as those of pregnancy). Such problems and decisions tend to be dynamic: actors enter into and leave the scene; patients change their minds; new tests and treatments become available; genetics professionals have to work together with a range of different professions across institutional boundaries and with the complexities of contemporary family life; and in any particular complex situation it is likely that a number of different and often competing values and commitments are going to be relevant. Against this background, the genetics professional needs nevertheless to work out, that is, make a judgement about, what is to count as good practice in a particular context and, because such practice is always to some extent provisional, partial, fluid and unstable, much of the day-to-day practice of genetics professionals will be taken up with what I have referred to as 'moral work'. I have suggested that such work is often effective at enabling acceptable 'solutions' to these problems to be worked out and the commitments underpinning good practice to be met. Sometimes, however, within the context of the care of particular patients and their families, everyday agreed and relatively unproblematic moral practices and commitments are transformed into *ethical* problems which unsettle the question of what it means to practice clinical genetics well and call for a different kind of work – for *ethics*. Such problems tend to persist. They have duration beyond the individual, particular case, and this is one reason why they get presented for deliberation at the Genethics Club. It is for this reason too, in part, that these are the kinds of problems I have largely been focusing on in this book.

Explaining the relationship between moral practices and ethics this way overlooks something important about moral craftsmanship, however. For the genetics professional who is committed to good practice and to the moral craft of genetics is not content to wait for the commitments and rules of thumb informing day-to-day practice to emerge as objects of ethical concern – that is, to see their role as merely responding to problems and stumbling blocks which present themselves in the

---

[16] Dewey, *Human Nature and Conduct.*

course of their work with patients and families.[17] The genetics professional committed to good practice is someone who takes problem-*seeking* seriously and sees the active seeking-out of moral and ethical problems as an important part of their commitment to moral 'craftsmanship'.[18] There are a number of reasons for this. One reason arises out of the genetics professional's recognition that the problems they encounter in their own day-to-day practice are inevitably to some extent contingent upon the kinds of patients and families they happen to see, the colleagues they happen to work with, and the difficulties they happen to come across. Even if, in practice, these problems frequently resonate with the experiences of genetics professionals elsewhere, the genetics professional committed to moral craftsmanship is not going to be satisfied with an approach which concentrates only on the resolution of ethical challenges or problems emergent in their day-to-day practice. To be satisfied with this would mean that a disproportionate role would be played by moral luck in the question of what is to count as an object of ethical concern.[19] While the genetics professional recognises the important role of such luck and acknowledges the value of those daily situations which prove unsettling of agreed and relatively stable practices, they view this as at best incomplete as an approach to ethics when committed to the moral craft of genetics.

The genetics professional committed to good practice is suspicious of approaches which take the moral and ethical problems of day-to-day practice at face value at least in part because of her awareness that much of this practice is unreflective. She is also aware of the potential for the 'moral work' which is so central to good practice to render invisible or to obscure important ethical issues, tensions and problems which might otherwise lead to the emergence of key practices and commitments as objects of ethical concern. An example of this was mentioned in passing earlier in this chapter in the situation in which a patient initially refused to share genetic information with her family members but where the moral work of the genetics professional – supporting, encouraging, and so on – ultimately meant that she did in fact do so. The patient's decision resolved the tension between the genetics professional's commitments to the care of the patient and to her family. Nevertheless, such situations have the potential to be troubling for the genetics professional because while on one interpretation her moral work has made good

---

[17] Sennet, *The Craftsman*; J. Ruskin, 'The Nature of Gothic', in J. Ruskin, *Unto this Last and Other Writings* (London: Penguin Books, 1997), pp. 77–110.
[18] Sennet, *The Craftsman*.
[19] B. Williams, *Ethics and the Limits of Philosophy* (London: Penguin Books, 2006), pp. 195–196.

practice possible, on another the very same moral work has rendered invisible an important moment in which what is to count as good practice might have emerged as a productive object of ethical concern – as an opportunity for critical reflection. The genetics professional is wary of approaches to good practice which identify ethics too closely with conflict, disagreement or the breakdown of consensus because there is a danger that in situations where there is broad agreement or where practice runs smoothly – perhaps because moral work has been successful – there may appear to be no important ethical issues to resolve, and no need to question or reflect critically upon such practice.

The genetics professional is also only too aware of the numerous examples of practices in medicine and elsewhere which were at one time widely agreed to be good practice, but which have subsequently come to be seen as highly problematic. An example of this in the context of medicine is the practice of refraining from informing terminally ill cancer patients about their prognosis on the grounds that this was in the patient's best interest. This was at one time standard practice but would now be seen to conflict with a commitment to patient-centredness which places much greater value on patients being fully informed.[20] The genetics professional is aware of the possibility that models of good practice can and do change and that what seems like good practice today may turn out to look very different tomorrow. It is not the fact of change or concern about moral luck itself which is the primary worry for genetics professionals, however. These are manifestations of a deeper concern. For the genetics professional concerned with the moral craft of genetics, the underlying problem with approaches to ethics which focus on conflict and disagreement, or on the contingencies of day-to-day practice, arises from her recognition that the fact that there is agreement about a particular practice – or that it has not so far emerged as unproblematic – does not in itself provide an answer to the question of whether such practice is good or right or morally praiseworthy. This means that the practices which are often most in need of critical reflection are precisely those that are widely seen as unproblematic, agreed and stable. Active problem-seeking is thus one of the key disciplines of moral craftsmanship for the genetics professional committed to good practice. For this reason, the genetics professional committed to moral craftsmanship places particular value on the active seeking-out of ethical problems. The genetics professional committed to doing a good job recognises the value of such problems. They recognise the value of developing the skills such as moral deliberation, critical reflection, and

---

[20] J. Katz, *The Silent World of Doctor and Patient* (New York: Free Press, 1984).

the skills of moral judgement associated with moral craftsmanship, and seek out opportunities for those skills to be tested and challenged.

Living morality

While problem-seeking is at the heart of the moral craft of genetics, any adequate account of the moral world of the genetics professional is also going to be one which recognises the importance of relatively stable and unproblematic unreflective practices and of the quotidian moral work by which they are sustained. The moral craftsman understands that problem-seeking only makes sense as an activity in the context of at least some relatively stable practices. Not everything can be a problem, not only because this would be undermining of good practice but also because problems make sense at all only in the context of broadly shared agreement in value judgements and in practices. Ethical objects of concern emerge against a background of moral agreement and shared views about the moral work of genetics and its value.

What this means, taken together, is that the genetics professional has to be skilled both at inhabiting the relatively stable, shared and unproblematised moral traditions underpinning good practice and skilled too at the problem-seeking through which such practices emerge as objects of ethical concern and as the subject of critical reflection. And this presents an important practical and ethical difficulty for the genetics professional committed to the moral craft of genetics. For how should the judgement be made about when one or the other of these is required? Under what kinds of circumstances and in what situations should the genetics professional continue to inhabit the relatively stable, unproblematic moral traditions constituting 'good practice' and when, in what kinds of contexts, should he or she view such practices as objects of ethical concern? This judgement is of real moral significance. For if the genetics professional is overly deferential to established, shared practices and habits and to their maintenance through moral work there is the risk of her practice becoming too conservative and unreflective, with all the implications discussed above. If, on the other hand, he or she adopts an approach which is too critical of established practice and experience, there is the danger of the breakdown of such practices and the loss of confidence in the value of experiential and implicit knowledge and expertise.[21] The cases presented for discussion at the Genethics Club suggest that there can be no single one-size-fits-all answer to the question of how such judgements are to be made and

---

[21] Williams, *Ethics and the Limits of Philosophy*, pp. 156–173.

can be no unambiguous rule of thumb by means of which this judgement is to be guided in particular cases. And this should come as no surprise. For, as the discussion in earlier chapters shows, there is no reason to believe that the emergence of the day-to-day practices, values and commitments by which good practice is informed as ethical objects of concern will be anything other than complex and highly contextual, and there is every reason to believe that good judgement in such contexts will greatly depend upon the embedded practical wisdom of the experienced genetics professional committed to the moral craft of genetics. It is clear that practices and commitments can emerge as potential objects of concern in many different ways and with multiple durations and intensities: often partial and incomplete, sometimes disappearing briefly only to re-emerge later in different form or in a somewhat transformed context. And it is against this background that the experienced genetics professional committed to good practice – aware of the importance both of unreflective practices and of critical reflection – is called upon to practice this aspect of her moral craftsmanship.

Wary of the lure of easy solutions, the experienced genetics professional committed to the moral craft of genetics sees an important and vital role in her practice for the continuation of an active and productive interplay between morals and ethics as a technique for ensuring that her practice is permeated by what might perhaps be thought of as a 'living morality' – a mode of engagement with practice which makes it possible for both ethics and morals to be taken seriously.[22] The genetics professional as moral craftsman recognises that while the commitments underpinning everyday good practice will sometimes emerge as ethical objects of concern in their own way and in their own time – prompted perhaps by the inherent instability of practice, because practice is always rather tentative or because moral work is only ever partially successful in particular cases – the sustainability and indeed the vitality of the living morality at the heart of moral craftsmanship depends upon the genetics professional's own commitment to the moral work of problem-seeking. This starts to suggest an answer to the question with which this chapter began. The question was: Why is it that the Genethics Club has been so popular with genetics professionals? Noting that genetics professionals initially come along to the Genethics Club because they have a particular problem, stumbling block or ethical issue they would like to discuss with colleagues, why do so many of them continue to attend again and again, in some cases for many years, long after their problem has been

---

[22] J. Glover, *Causing Death and Saving Lives* (London: Penguin Books, 1977), pp. 26–29; Sennett, *The Craftsman*, pp. 214–238.

resolved? It has been clear to me over the time that I have been involved in this work that the genetics professionals who attend Genethics Club share a deep commitment to doing their job well for its own sake and that they recognise that this requires a commitment not only to good practice in the medical aspects of their day-to-day practice but also in what I have referred to as the 'moral craft' of genetics.[23] Against this background commitment to moral craftsmanship, the discussion in this chapter and particularly in the last few pages, has begun to hint at a rather surprising answer to the question of why genetics professionals continue to attend Genethics Club. It suggests that while genetics professionals might initially attend because they are looking for solutions, the reason they stay is because of a growing recognition of the importance of problems in the development and practice of moral craftsmanship. For the genetics professionals committed to good practice, the Genethics Club has become valuable as a social space not only for the achievement of solutions but also a space for the *production* of problems. The genetics professional attends the Genethics Club because they recognise its value as a way of keeping their practice open and of working to maintain a sustainable living morality. The Genethics Club is a place not only of discussion and deliberation but is also a technique for the unsettling of everyday, established stable practices in productive ways which facilitate moral craftsmanship and the emergence of the practical wisdom at the heart of good practice.

---

[23] It is important to make the point here that the discussion in this chapter, and indeed in the book as a whole, is not intended to suggest that the Genethics Club is the only place in which moral craftsmanship does or could happen. For more on this, see Chapter 7.

7   Methodological reflections

For almost as long as there has been bioethics, there have been demands for it to be more empirically informed and for a greater emphasis to be placed on the role of the empirical in bioethical deliberation.[1] These demands have taken a number of different forms, ranging from relatively straightforward pleas for the greater use of empirical evidence to enrich philosophical bioethics[2] all the way through to demands for fully-integrated 'hermeneutic' approaches.[3] Of particular interest in the present context are the arguments that have been made for the development of ethnographic approaches to bioethics.[4] One influential example

[1] R.C. Fox and J.P. Swazey, 'Examining American bioethics: its problems and prospects' (2005) 14 *Cambridge Quarterly of Healthcare Ethics*, 361–373; R.C. Fox and J.P. Swazey, *Observing Bioethics* (Oxford University Press, 2008); B. Hoffmaster and C. Hooker, 'How experience confronts ethics' (2009) 23 *Bioethics*, 4, 214–225; G. Widdershoven, T. Abma and B. Molewijk, 'Empirical ethics as dialogical practice' (2009) 23 *Bioethics*, 4, 236–248; W. Shelton, 'Empirical bioethics: present and future possibilities' (2009) 9 *American Journal of Bioethics*, 6–7, 74–75; K. Hoeyer, ' "Ethics wars": reflections on the antagonism between bioethicists and social science observers of biomedicine' (2006) 29 *Human Studies*, 203–227; R.C. Fox, 'Advanced medical technology – social and ethical implications' (1976) 2 *Annual Review of Sociology*, 231–268; B. Hoffmaster, 'Can ethnography save the life of medical ethics?' (1992) 35 *Social Science and Medicine*, 12, 1421–1432; R.G. de Vries, 'Toward a sociology of bioethics' (1995) 18 *Qualitative Sociology*, 1, 119–128; A. Hope, 'Empirical medical ethics' (1999) *Journal of Medical Ethics*, 219–220; B. Hoffmaster (ed.) *Bioethics in Social Context* (Philadelphia: Temple University Press, 2001); R.A. Carson, 'Interpretive bioethics: the way of discernment' (1990) 11 *Theoretical Medicine and Bioethics*, 51–60; M. Dunn, M. Sheehan, T. Hope and M. Parker, 'Towards methodological innovation in empirical ethics research' (in press) *Cambridge Quarterly of Healthcare Ethics*.
[2] A.A. Kon, 'The role of empirical research in bioethics' (2009) 6 *American Journal of Bioethics*, 3, 59–65; Hope, 'Empirical medical ethics'; J. McMillan and A. Hope, 'The possibility of empirical psychiatric ethics', in G. Widdershoven, T. Hope, J. McMillan and L. van der Scheer (eds.) *Empirical Ethics in Psychiatry* (Oxford University Press, 2008), pp. 9–22.
[3] Widdershoven, Abma and Molewijk, 'Empirical ethics as dialogical practice'; L. van der Scheer and G. Widdershoven, 'Integrated empirical ethics: loss of normativity?' (2004) 7 *Medicine, Health Care and Philosophy*, 71–79.
[4] P.A. Marshall, 'Anthropology and bioethics' (1992) 6 *Medical Anthropology Quarterly*, 1, 49–73; J.H. Muller, 'Anthropology, bioethics and medicine: a provocative trilogy' (1994) 8 *Medical Anthropology Quarterly*, 4, 448–467; A. Kleinman,

of this is Arthur Kleinman's call for the incorporation of ethnographic methods into bioethics on the grounds that it – bioethics – lacks what Clifford Geertz, following the analytic philosopher Gilbert Ryle, refers to as 'thick description'.[5] Kleinman argues that, in its most common forms, even in many of those informed by empirical research, bioethics fails to take sufficiently seriously the moral significance of the realities within which people, including patients, families and doctors live and work.[6] This is an important failing, he believes, because he agrees with Geertz that it is *meaning* which counts in the analysis of such realities:

> The concept of culture I espouse … is essentially a semiotic one. Believing, with Max Weber, that man is an animal suspended in webs of significance he himself has spun, I take culture to be those webs, and the analysis of it to be therefore not an experimental science in search of law but an interpretive one in search of meaning.[7]

For Kleinman, the failure of bioethics to pay sufficient attention to meaning and culture has the implication that its attempts to apply ethical principles are likely to be insensitive to morally significant features of its object of concern.[8] By means of thick descriptions of how those who live in these worlds make sense of their own lives and their interactions with those of others around them,[9] ethnography offers the possibility of a bioethics better informed about the meaning and intersubjective significance of the situation under consideration and of the local 'worlds of experience' within which and in relation to which bioethical issues arise.[10] From this naturalistic perspective the ethnographer's task is to

---

Writing at the Margin: Discourse Between Anthropology and Medicine (Berkeley: University of California Press, 1997); A. Kleinman, 'Moral experience and ethical reflection: Can ethnography reconcile them? A quandary for "the new bioethics" ' (1999) 128 *Daedalus*, 4, 69–97; C. Bosk, 'Professional ethicist available: logical, secular, friendly' (1999) 128 *Daedalus*, 47–68; C. Bosk, 'Irony, ethnography, and informed consent', in B. Hoffmaster (ed.) *Bioethics in Social Context* (Philadelphia: Temple University Press, 2001), pp. 199–220; D.S. Davis, 'Rich cases: The ethics of thick description' (1991) 21 *Hastings Center Report*, 4, 12–17; B. Jennings, 'Ethics and ethnography in neonatal intensive care', in G. Weisz (ed.) *Social Science Perspectives on Medical Ethics* (Philadelphia University of Pennsylvania Press, 1990), pp. 261–272; C. Bosk, *What Would You Do? Juggling Bioethics and Ethnography* (University of Chicago Press, 2008).

[5] C. Geertz, *The Interpretation of Cultures* (New York: Basic Books, 1973); G. Ryle, 'The thinking of thoughts: What is "le Penseur" doing?', in G. Ryle, *Collected Papers II: Collected Essays 1929–1968* (London: Hutchinson, 1971).

[6] Kleinman, 'Moral experience and ethical reflection'.

[7] Geertz, *The Interpretation of Cultures*, p. 5.

[8] Kleinman, *Writing at the Margin*, p. 48.

[9] M. Hammersley and P. Atkinson, *Ethnography: Principles in Practice* (London: Routledge, 2006), p. 6; Hoffmaster, *Bioethics in Social Context*, pp. 4–5.

[10] Kleinman, 'Moral experience', p. 70.

understand the situated rationality of the context within which people's actions *make sense*.

It is through ongoing interaction and a developing relationship with the individuals and groups who belong to the milieu being explored that the researcher enters ever-more deeply – psychologically and interpersonally, as well as intellectually – into its social structure and culture and the experiences, personae, and lives of those who people it.[11]

The claim here is that it is (only) possible to come to understand what is involved for people themselves, i.e. to perceive local 'webs of significance' by spending significant extended periods of time in the setting: participating, talking to people, observing what goes on, studying documentary sources, exploring the meaningful roles of material objects, and collecting other meaningful features of the setting – that is, through participant observation.[12] In achieving this, the ethnographer relies to some extent upon the everyday epistemological skills of social actors.

Fortunately, the capacities we have developed as social actors can give us such access. As participant observers we can learn the culture or subculture of the people we are studying. We can come to interpret the world in the same way as they do, and thereby learn to understand their behaviour in a different way to that in which natural scientists set about understanding the behaviour of physical phenomena.[13]

In these ways, it is argued, ethnographers and, through them, bioethicists, can begin to get a 'thick' sense of the worlds of the social actors under consideration.

Much of the situated rationality of interest to ethnographers will inevitably be moral. For when an ethnographer studies kinship relations, the role of 'gifts', or 'signals of regard', and so on, these will in very many cases be seen to be productive, implicitly or explicitly, of entitlements, obligations, rights, duties, or of conceptions of what it means to live well. Kleinman himself goes further than this, arguing that local experiences are *fundamentally* moral.[14]

Why moral? Because they consist of the contestations and compromises that actualize values both for collectives and for individuals. Indeed, the individual-collective dichotomy is overdone; within these social processes values

[11] R.C. Fox, 'Observations and reflections of a perpetual fieldworker' (2004) 595 *Annals of the American Academy*, 314.
[12] Geertz, *The Interpretation of Cultures*; Bosk, *What Would You Do?*
[13] Hammersley and Atkinson, *Ethnography*, p. 8.
[14] Kleinman, *Writing at the Margin*, pp. 44–45.

are negotiated and reworked among others in a space that is thoroughly intersubjective.[15]

The value of ethnography for bioethics then is that it offers methods for coming to understand and for making sense of these moral experiences, fragmentary and lacking in coherence as they may be, from 'within', by providing a way of entering into these social spaces. And if the subject matter of ethnography is taken, as Kleinman argues it must be, to be the actualization of values in the everyday situated negotiations of meanings, then all ethnography is, in effect, to be conceptualized as *moral* ethnography.[16]

Having placed particular emphasis on the value of the ethnographer's grasp of local moral practices for bioethics, Kleinman goes on to introduce a distinction between the ethnographer's concern with the *moral* and the bioethicist's concern with the *ethical*. In this distinction, the moral (the concern of the ethnographer) consists of the actual commitments, compromises and practices by means of which social participants negotiate what is at stake locally, and ethics (the concern of the bioethicist) is a universalising, principled or codified body of abstract knowledge about the definition and realisation of the good.[17] In making this distinction, Kleinman is not claiming that the moral is more important than the ethical. Indeed, in his own writing – in common with many other ethnographers – he places a great deal of emphasis on the ethical and the application of 'universal standards', e.g. in his critique of practices in Rwanda and Bosnia. His purpose in making the distinction between morals and ethics is rather to draw attention to a methodological problem faced by bioethics and to the contribution moral ethnography might make to overcoming it. He argues that, in order to be coherent and adequate to its task bioethics needs to develop both a method for 'accounting for local moral experience *and* a method of applying ethical deliberation' and he sees this as a challenge bioethics will only be able to meet if it incorporates complementary ethnographic methods.[18]

[B]ioethics is confronted with an extraordinarily difficult quandary: how to reconcile the clearly immense differences in the social and personal realities of moral life with the need to apply a universal standard to those fragments of experience that can foster not only comparison and evaluation but also action.

---

[15] Kleinman, 'Moral experience', p. 71.
[16] See also A. Dzur, 'Democratizing the hospital: deliberative-democratic bioethics' (2002) 27 *Journal of Health Politics, Policy and Law*, 2, 177–211.
[17] Kleinman, *Writing at the Margin*, p. 45.
[18] Kleinman, 'Moral experience', p. 69.

For philosophers, the gulf between the universal and the particular may be regarded as an irksome and a perennial barrier; but bioethicists, like clinicians and policy implementers, simply cannot function without finding a way of relating ethical deliberation to local [moral] contexts.[19]

An effective bioethics, Kleinman argues, will be one capable of taking both local, networked, moral experience *and* universal, transcendent ethical 'standards' into account,[20] and his call for a complementary and constructive relationship between bioethics and ethnography is intended to lead to the development of just such a methodologically coherent and empirically rich approach to the ethical and moral dimensions of medicine and health care.

Broadly similar calls for the incorporation of complementary ethnographic methods into bioethics have also been made by a number of other prominent ethnographers.[21] However, the positing of a complementarity between bioethics and ethnography is not unproblematic as a response to the separation of the ethical and empirical because the concept of 'complementarity' implies the very distinction it is intended to overcome. Bioethics and ethnography can only be coherently conceptualised as *complementary* and bioethics only be said to be *in need of* ethnography insofar as disciplinary distinctions are held to exist between those concerned with the ethical and those concerned with the moral and insofar as they can be considered to be concerned with radically different objects. There are a number of reasons for being sceptical of these distinctions.

First, ethnography has throughout its history often been implicitly 'ethical' – whether in the sense that it was associated with a 'body of abstract knowledge held by experts about "the good" and ways to realize it';[22] in its associations with colonialism;[23] or more recently in its perception of itself as having a duty to represent or to ensure a voice to marginalised or vulnerable groups.[24] In this respect, ethnography has

---

[19] *Ibid.*, p. 70.   [20] *Ibid.*, p. 69.

[21] Marshall, 'Anthropology and bioethics'; Muller, 'Anthropology, bioethics and medicine'; Kleinman, *Writing at the Margin*; Kleinman, 'Moral experience'. Bosk, 'Professional ethicist available'; Bosk, 'Irony, ethnography, and informed consent'; Davis, 'Rich cases: The ethics of thick description'; Jennings, 'Ethics and ethnography in neonatal intensive care'; Bosk, *What Would You Do?*.

[22] Kleinman, *Writing at the Margin*, p. 45.

[23] P. Pels, 'Professions of duplexity: a prehistory of ethical codes in anthropology' (1999) 40 *Current Anthropology*, 2, 101–136.

[24] N. Scheper-Hughes, 'The primacy of the ethical: propositions for a militant anthropology' (1995) 36 *Current Anthropology*, 3, 409–440; G.E. Marcus and M.M.J. Fischer, *Anthropology as Cultural Critique: An Experimental Moment in the Human Sciences* (University of Chicago Press, 1986).

frequently embodied the ethical in its approach to the moral.[25] What this suggests is that, whatever else the incorporation of ethnography into bioethics might do, it cannot be coherently thought of as the *complementing* of ethical deliberation with (non-ethical) empirical, moral, richness.

Second, and relatedly, the fact that ethnography is in its very methodological self-understanding, a fundamentally *interpretive* enterprise means that what it brings to bioethics cannot be disentangled from values or ethics even when it is not being explicitly 'ethical'.[26] This is at least part of the point intended to be captured by the concept of 'reflexivity'.

Reflexivity ... implies that the orientations of researchers will be shaped by their socio-historical locations, including the values and interests that these locations confer upon them. What this represents is a rejection of the idea that social research is, or can be, carried out in some autonomous realm that is insulated from the wider society and from the particular biography of the researcher.[27]

Third, and perhaps most importantly in the present context, what the cases discussed in the earlier chapters of this book serve to highlight is the fact that the conceptualisation of the situated rationality of local experience and of practices as fundamentally moral, and of the epistemological project of the ethnographer in terms of the description of these moral practices, is also itself deeply problematic. In particular, the description of culture as fundamentally moral is too *thin*. Many cultures, such as that of the Genethics Club, for example, or even that of ethnography itself (as the concept of reflexivity shows), involve and in some cases are constituted by, *interplay* between the moral and the ethical.[28] The identification of the empirical with the moral – where the moral is itself identified with relatively unproblematic day-to-day normalised practices and commitments (even if these are practices of contestation) – must inevitably fail to capture the ethico-moral complexity of forms of everyday life in which consideration of 'the values, rules of conduct and character traits which are involved in right action, doing

[25] P. Pels, 'Professions of duplexity'; van der Sheer and Widdershoven, 'Integrated empirical ethics'; Bosk, *What Would You Do?*, p. 240; L. Turner, 'Anthropological and sociological critiques of bioethics' (2009) 6 *Bioethical Inquiry*, 83–98.

[26] Geertz, *Interpretation of Cultures*, p. 5; Turner, 'Anthropological and sociological critiques of bioethics'.

[27] Hammersley and Atkinson, *Ethography*, p. 16.

[28] Muller, 'Anthropology, bioethics and medicine'.

good, and living well' – that is, ethics[29] – plays a significant role and in which local experiences are as a consequence fundamentally ethico-moral rather than moral. What the discussion in previous chapters – and in particular that in Chapter 6 – suggests, I think, is that a more interesting, productive and plausible way to conceptualise the relationship between ethics and morals might be to think of the moral as the commonly shared, normalised practices and values which structure everyday life, and the ethical as constituted by situations in which, and by the extent to which, the moral emerges as problematic, contested, in need of deliberation, analysis or critique. Something like this account, to which I return again later in this chapter, in which the ethical is conceptualised as the enactment of the moral as problematic has the advantage of making a richer account of both morality and of ethics, and of the interplay between them possible, and also has the advantage of making visible the ways in which ethics is enacted (or not) in practices. On this account, the methodological problem of how best to understand the relationship between the moral and the ethical becomes one shared by both the bioethicist and the ethnographer.[30]

While Kleinman and other ethnographers are I think right to call for activity at the interface between bioethics and ethnography, whatever ethnography brings to the table will not come free of ethics, values or morals. Ethnography is, like bioethics, a practice situated in and concerned with ethico-moral 'webs of significance'. The incorporation of ethnography into bioethics will therefore not be coherently achieved by conceptualising this as the *complementing* of ethical deliberation with empirical richness. Any coherent response to the problem of how to understand the enfolding of ethics and morals will require the development of new ethico-ethnographic methods for the investigation of genuinely ethico-moral objects.[31]

The ethics of ethnography

Having considered calls for the use of ethnography to complement bioethics, I want now to explore moves in the opposite direction, i.e. calls for increasing attention to be paid to the ethical dimensions of

[29] R.E. Ashcroft, 'Ethical issues in statistical genetics', in D.J. Balding, M.J. Bishop and C. Cannings (eds.) *Handbook of Statistical Genetics*, third edition (Chichester: John Wiley and Sons, 2007), pp. 1325–1345.

[30] M. Parker, 'Deliberative bioethics', in R.E. Ashcroft, A. Dawson, H. Draper and J. McMillan (eds.) *Principles of Health Care Ethics*, second edition (Chichester: John Wiley and Sons, 2007), pp. 185–191.

[31] J. Law and J. Urry, 'Enacting the social' (2004) 33 *Economy and Society*, 3, 390–410.

ethnographic research. These have arisen as a result both of internal debate within the social sciences – within anthropology in particular – and also because of the influence of developments outside of the social sciences, most notably those in the regulation of medical research. From inside anthropology, the theoretical and regulatory turn to ethics has grown out of an acknowledgement that anthropology's own history has been, and continues to be, value-driven (by colonialism, by the obligations of 'representation', and so on), and that ethnographic research has implications for the communities it studies. The ethical turn in anthropology – and in the social sciences more broadly – has also however been driven by important cultural shifts outside these disciplines, notably by developments in the regulation of medicine and medical research. Changes in the regulation of medicine have had profound and wide-ranging implications for research in other disciplines, including in the social sciences. The Nuremberg Code and the Declaration of Helsinki, for example, which were developed because of concerns about medical research, have led to a broad expectation that all researchers carrying out research involving human participants, whatever their discipline, should submit their research protocols for consideration by an ethics committee.[32] The form of the ethical turn in the social sciences has also been affected by the substantive ethical issues arising in medical ethics, notably the requirement to obtain 'informed consent' from research participants prior to the commencement of the research.[33]

Driven to some extent by each of these sets of forces, increasing attention has been paid to the ethics of ethnography by professional associations and funding bodies relevant to ethnographic research.[34] For example, the American Anthropological Association, the Association of Social Anthropology of the UK and the Commonwealth, the British Sociological Association and the Economic and Social Research Council have all in recent years developed codes of ethics or ethical 'frameworks'.[35] There has however been a great deal of resistance among

---

[32] M. Strathern, 'Accountability and ethnography', in M. Strathern (ed.) *Audit Culture: Anthropological Studies in Accountability, Ethics, and the Academy* (London: Routledge, 2000), pp. 279–304.

[33] M. Boulton and M. Parker, 'Informed consent in a changing environment' (2007) 65 *Social Science and Medicine*, 2187–2198.

[34] C. Fluehr-Lobban, *Ethics and the Profession of Anthropology: Dialogue for Ethically Conscious Practice*, second edition (Walnut Creek: AltaMira Press, 2003).

[35] American Anthropological Association, *Code of Ethics* (American Anthropological Association, 1998) available at www.aaanet.org (accessed 1 August 2011); Association of Social Anthropologists of the UK and the Commonwealth, *Ethical Guidelines for Good Research Practice* (London: Association of Social Anthropologists of the UK and the Commonwealth, 1999) available at www.theasa.org/ethics (accessed 1 August 2011); British Sociological Association, *Statement of Ethical Practice* (London: British

ethnographers to the development of professional codes of ethics and to the idea that ethnographic research should be subject to ethical review by ethics committees on the same terms as medical research.[36] Some of this resistance has been grounded in arguments that the potential harms associated with ethnography are nothing like of the same order as those associated with clinical research in medicine.[37] Others have focused on claims about the inappropriateness of the medical model of bioethics that ethnographers have been forced to follow and in particular the stress it places on the importance of prior informed consent as a mechanism for respecting and protecting the interests of those with whom the research is to be carried out. The concerns ethnographers have about the approaches to informed consent used in medical research are related to the fact that it has tended to be interpreted in *anticipatory* terms, i.e. based on the idea that implications of the research, its methodology and research questions can be anticipated, discussed and agreed to before the research has begun. Marilyn Strathern, for one, has argued that this is itself unethical.

This could, I suggest, hold a new way of being demeaning to informants. It pushes the exploratory, indeterminate and unpredictable nature of social relations (between ethnographer and his or her third party) back onto a 'point of production', with the ethnographer as initiator. However much talk there is of collaboration or of conserving the autonomy of subjects or recognizing their input into the research or taking power into account, this aspect of ethics in advance, of anticipate negotiations, belittles the creative power of social relations.[38]

It is clear that such concerns do not arise because ethnographers consider consent, or ethics more broadly, to be unimportant aspects of research practice. Indeed, ethnographers have, as evidenced by the growing literature in this area, themselves become increasingly preoccupied with the need to involve, respect and appropriately represent host communities, and with the ethical dimensions of the ethnographic research methods they use. The problem with the adoption of such professional codes and with the deliberations of ethical committees for ethnographers is that they fail to recognise that the ethics of consent

---

Sociological Association, 2002) available at www.britsoc.co.uk (accessed 1 October 2006); Economic and Social Research Council, *Research Ethics Framework* (Economic and Social Research Council, 2006) available at www.esrc.ac.uk (accessed 1 August 2011).

[36] Pels, 'Professions of duplexity'.

[37] E. Murphy and R. Dingwall, 'Informed consent, anticipatory regulation and ethnographic practice' (2007) 65 *Social Science and Medicine*, 11, 2223–2234.

[38] Strathern, 'Accountability and ethnography', p. 295.

needs to be thought of differently in ethnography, where the research undertaken is based upon the tentative development of research questions and analysis in the context of emergent relationships of trust. At the heart of these concerns is a belief that within the context of ethnography the obtaining of consent from those with whom the research is to be pursued must involve developmental and creative processes incompatible with the concept of *anticipatory* informed consent.

Ethnographic consent is a relational and sequential process rather than a contractual agreement and lasts throughout the period of research ... Typically, at the start of such research, consent is both tentative and limited and the researcher's access to sensitive aspects of the setting may be restricted. Over time, as the trust between the researcher and host develops, access may be granted to previously restricted areas or interactions.[39]

Increasingly, ethnographers have argued that appropriate consent can only be achieved through an ongoing and developmental *negotiation* of the relationship between researcher and research hosts.

[W]e need an investigation of the possibility of an emergent ethics, one which is no longer tied to a specific community (such as a professional association) but which locates ethical discussion in the negotiation of individual or communal interests that is characteristic of the practice of fieldwork.[40]

The concept of 'negotiation' is itself not unproblematic as a basis for the identification and addressing of ethical issues in ethnography, however. One reason for this is that, given the emphasis in ethnography on cultural difference, the notion of negotiation inevitably begs questions about the extent to which the meaning of what is being negotiated can in fact be established prior to the completion of the ethnographic research. This is an important methodological consideration, for if the purpose of negotiation between the researcher and the researched is to reach agreement about what is to constitute ethical research practice, it will be essential for some degree of intersubjective understanding to be possible about what is meant by, for example, an 'ethical consideration'. The ethnographer's methodological assumption that such understanding is not possible without thick description – which underpins its critique of bioethics – means that, from within this practice, the possibility of negotiation about 'ethics' cannot be taken for granted. This is because it is not easy to see how the ethnographer (or the member of

---

[39] Murphy and Dingwall, 'Informed consent, anticipatory regulation and ethnographic practice'.

[40] P. Pels, 'The trickster's dilemma: ethics and the technologies of the anthropological self', in M. Strathern (ed.) *Audit Culture: Anthropological Studies in Accountability, Ethics, and the Academy* (London: Routledge, 2000), p. 163.

the community hosting the research) can be confident about just *what* it is that is under negotiation. A further and related reason why the concept of a negotiated solution to the problem of ethics in ethnography is problematic is because in addition to it being unclear *what* exactly is being negotiated, it is also going to be difficult for the parties to be confident about the meaning of the processes of negotiation themselves. That is, it is not going to be clear, for any of the parties concerned, what it means for the other to 'negotiate' and 'reach agreement'. The social spaces within which negotiation about what matters locally takes place and within which cultural conflicts are resolved are precisely those which are presupposed by the ethnographer to be radically different between cultures and in need of interpretation on the basis of extended fieldwork. These two points are not unrelated of course, partly because both concern the possibility of emerging understanding and of shared meanings about what it means to carry out ethical research, but also because taken together they make it clear that *what* is under negotiation, that is 'ethics', will be shaped by the *how* of negotiation, that is 'method', and vice versa.

In the first part of this chapter, I argued that the incorporation of ethnography into bioethics could not coherently be thought of as the complementing of ethical deliberation with empirical richness, but had to be seen as requiring both the development of new forms of ethico-ethnographic knowledge production and the reconceptualisation of the relationship between the ethical and the moral. In this second part, I have reached a strikingly similar conclusion in response to calls for the incorporation of ethics into ethnography. An adequate and appropriate approach to both the ethnography of ethics and the ethics of ethnography will be one which acknowledges that, in the negotiations between the researcher and the researched, it is not going to be possible to separate the *what* of negotiation from its *how*. Negotiation requires the object of the research, its method and its ethics to all be up for grabs.

The liminal and the duplex

Anthropologists have sometimes theorised ethnography as a 'liminal' discipline positioned astride, or perhaps creating, a threshold between moral cultures.[41]

---

[41] Kleinman, 'Moral experience'; Hammersley and Atkinson, *Ethnography*; C. Fluehr-Lobban, 'Globalization of research and international standards of ethics in anthropology' (2000) 925 *Annals of the New York Academy of Sciences*, 37–44.

Ethnography is a method of knowledge production by which the ethnographer enters into the ordinary, everyday space of moral processes in a local world. The ethnographer, no matter how successful she is in participant observation, either is or becomes an outsider – even if she begins as an indigenous member of the community she studies. She feels the tug of local obligations and the push of local practices, but for all of that she is never so completely absorbed by what is most at stake for community members that their world of experience is entirely hers.[42]

It is an implication of the arguments presented thus far in this chapter that the concept of 'liminality', when thought of as 'standing at the threshold between two worlds', does not go far enough towards capturing the productive implications of folding ethics and ethnography together. In response to something like these considerations, Peter Pels argues for a more radical position than that of liminality, one he refers to as *duplexity*.[43]

Like the archaeologists confronted with a Hopi scholar telling them a story with a moral, ethnographers are bound to acknowledge the moral 'duplexity' of research: the fact that engagement with people living in one's field of study requires one to negotiate 'other' values instead of implicitly assuming that our principles of ethics and expertise are universal.[44]

An ethnographic role is duplex for Pels when it requires not only acknowledgement of the ethical dimensions of the liminal positioning of ethnography, but also recognition of the fact that what must be negotiated in cross-cultural encounters is both the ethics of the research *and* its modes of knowledge production. Pels suggests that a resolution of the problem of enfolding ethics and ethnography in research might be found in the intersubjective and interdisciplinary negotiation of what such research is to *become*.

Thus, we have come full circle: rethinking ethics implies rethinking expertise, and that implies rethinking modernity as well: as something that emanates not from 'us' but from interaction. We should locate ethics not in a Kantian, law-like universal nor in the postmodernist 'moral self' whose ethical relation to the elusive other we can only take on trust, but in concrete practise of interaction with others.[45]

---

[42] Kleinman, 'Moral experience', p. 77.

[43] Pels, 'Professions of duplexity'; L. Meskell and P. Pels (eds.) *Embedding Ethics* (Oxford: Berg, 2005); P. Pels, ' "Where there aren't no ten commandments": redefining ethics during the Darkness in El Dorado scandal', in L. Meskell and P. Pels (eds.) *Embedding Ethics* (Oxford: Berg, 2005), pp. 69–99.

[44] Meskell and Pels, *Embedding Ethics*, p. 8.

[45] *Ibid.*, pp. 8–9.

Duplexity is an approach in which there is an interactive fusion of ethics and method in the intersubjective and interdisciplinary actualisation of the values of research, and in which the negotiation of ethics cannot be separated from questions of methodology.

The fusion of ethics and method ... seems to promise to constitute the scientific subject as an ethical one immediately, rather than by proxy that entails a tendency to dissemble the expert 'self' from the practice of research as such.[46]

While Pels's duplex position comes much closer than that of liminality to resolving the relationship between ethics and ethnography in ways compatible with the arguments discussed above, the concept of 'duplexity' still has significant limitations as a way of theorising the relation between ethnography and ethics. For, while Pels's intention is to replace the disciplinary separation of ethics and ethnography with an emergent ethico-ethnographic method grounded in negotiation, he remains committed to the methodological centrality of radical cultural difference and this means that, in the end, the concept of duplexity can do little more than redescribe the problem.

[T]he primary moral engagement of fieldwork is the negotiation of different moral complexes with each other. The necessity of living with double standards – in duplexity – signifies a moral topography of differences that pertains everywhere – not only among Yanomami but also when we study a biogenics company, participate in the definition of an archaeological site, or try to get used to the linguistic conventions of an internal review board.[47]

I want to argue that since the late 19th century anthropology's epistemological commitment to cultural difference has made its morals essentially duplex: without duplicitous intention or moral corruption, anthropologists cannot but adopt 'double standards'.[48]

The arguments I presented earlier in this chapter regarding the necessary conditions for meaningful negotiation suggest that it is not going to be possible to take ethics seriously without putting the commitment to cultural difference at risk. For any resolution of the relationship between ethics and ethnography will need to be one which involves the problematising of both ethics and method in an intersubjective commitment to making moral and methodological sense *across such difference*. This implies the possibility of an emergent shared understanding between the researcher and researched about both ethics and method in which each is shaped by the other. That is, it is an approach in which

---

[46] *Ibid.*, p. 22.   [47] *Ibid.*, pp. 93–94.
[48] Pels, 'Professions of duplexity', p. 102.

the 'creative power of social relations' is reaffirmed.[49] This is not to suggest that cultural difference is unimportant but it is to argue that in the enfolding of ethics and ethnography something *new* and *shared* is created and this requires that the interplay between researcher and researched be conceptualised not simply as the resultant of the combination of differences nor simply as the recognition and valuing of difference, but rather as involving the joint creation of something new. Something new means that the old 'parts' are properly transformed.

It would be difficult to overestimate the methodological impact of the concept of negotiation in this context. For in addition to emphasising the creative power of social relations across difference, it also brings with it another significant challenge. The challenge arises because the shared understandings required for such negotiation to work as the mode of engagement at the heart of ethical research practice will themselves be in large measure ethical. One way into this is as follows. When ethnographers call for a negotiational approach to ethics (rather than one based in professional codes, or in abstract principles), they implicitly acknowledge that there are *non*-negotiational methods by which ethico-methodological issues might be resolved. This raises the question of just what it is that makes negotiation better than other available approaches to ethical research practice in ethnography, and this is at least in part an *ethical* question. While this is not the place to pursue this discussion very far, it is clear that the call for negotiation is only going to be capable of doing the normative work required of it in association within a constellation of other ethical concepts. What, for example, does it mean to say that an ethnographer should negotiate with her host community? Would the threat of violence if the host community did not cooperate with the research constitute negotiation? If not, what is it that marks the significant difference between the threat of violence and negotiation? At this point it becomes clear that cross-cultural engagement with thick ethical (rather than moral) concepts such as for example 'recognition', 'respect', 'justice', 'dignity', 'harm' and so on begins to look unavoidable for the possibility of any ethico-ethnography. And if these concepts are to be capable of delineating the ethical conditions for ethico-ethnographic method in the context of cross-cultural negotiation, they must be capable of moving across cultural and practice boundaries. And for this to be possible they must be a very special kind of object indeed. Just as it proved impossible to import ethnography into ethics without changing both the method and its object, so too has it proved in relation to the importing of ethics into ethnography. The importing of ethics,

---

[49] Strathern, 'Accountability and ethnography', p. 295.

as negotiation, into ethnographic research turns such research into an *intervention* involving the negotiation of ethics and method with the research hosts and, in this intervention, it is not going to be possible to avoid cross-cultural engagement with ethical concepts such as those mentioned above. This inevitably puts the assumption of radical cultural difference at the heart of the ethnographic method at risk.

Researching ethics as an object of concern

I have argued that the folding together of the ethical and the ethnographic in empirical bioethics research requires the development of new ethico-ethnographic methods for the investigation of ethico-moral objects. What might this mean in practice?

Drawing upon discussion in previous chapters and in particular upon the account of moral craftsmanship developed in Chapter 6, I have conceptualised the moral as comprising those commonly shared, relatively normalised practices, values and commitments which – in the context of a significant amount of *moral work* – constitute and structure the majority of everyday practice in clinical genetics. I have conceptualised the ethical, by contrast, as those occasions on which these everyday practices create ethical problems around moral commitments and in relation to the practices associated with them. An example of this is the cluster of ethical problems created by the construction, validation and clinical use of the family pedigree and the consequent transformation of the genetics professional's commitment to the 'patient in the family' into a commitment to the 'patient in the families', which was introduced in Chapter 2 and further illustrated in Chapter 3. These are occasions on which moral commitments are transformed into ethical *problems*. Importantly, this account of the relationship between morals and ethics is not one in which ethical problems *emerge* in the course of day-to-day moral practices but is, in contrast, one in which everyday practices *create* ethical problems around what are otherwise relatively stable and unproblematic moral commitments. It is an implication of this account that clinical genetics is *inherently* ethical and that even though solutions may often be found to particular ethical problems, there can be no *closure to* or *resolution of* the problem – and the transformational potential – of the 'ethics of genetics'. It is the everyday practices of clinical genetics themselves which create ethical problems in relation to the important moral commitments of genetics professionals. This account of the relationship between morals and ethics, in which the ethical is conceptualised as the enactment of the moral *by practices* as problematic, has the advantage of making possible a richer account of both ethics and morals, of the interplay between them, and of the potential for such interplay to open up practice and make new kinds of encounters with experience possible. It is in this context that the attractions of the practice of 'problem-seeking' – as a way of opening up practices – for the genetics professional committed to the moral craft of genetics make sense and here too that the genetics professional's enthusiasm for the Genethics Club as a technique for the encouragement of productive interplay between the ethical and the moral, and for the fostering of moral *craftsmanship*, becomes understandable.

What are the other implications of this account of the relationships between the moral and the ethical for the enfolding of ethics and the ethnographic in bioethics research methods? One of its main implications is that such research requires careful attention to be paid to the phenomena – the ethico-moral objects – described above. That is, to the interplay between ethics and morals, to the ways in which everyday practices create ethical problems around otherwise unproblematic moral commitments, to the forms and uses of moral craftsmanship and moral work, and to the judgements made and controversies about when one or the other of these is called for. Something which has been apparent in the cases discussed throughout this book – but particularly those in Chapter 5, perhaps – is the fact that the emergence of ethical problems in these kinds of ways takes time. Problems have duration; some things change, others endure, and this too has implications for research. For, it suggests that bioethics research which seeks to enfold ethics and the empirical is going to require special importance to be placed on the tracking of the *forms*, *uses* and *trajectories* of these ethico-moral objects – the creation of ethical problems, the interplay between ethics and morals, the uses of moral work, and the practices of problem-seeking and moral craftsmanship – over time and across different communities of practice. It will, that is, see the mapping of the biographies of such objects as deserving of particular attention.[50]

Research coherently enfolding the ethical and the ethnographic will be characterised by the creative, intersubjective negotiation of both method and ethics by the researcher and the researched. This has the implication that such research will – in its tracking of ethics – take the methodological form of an *intervention*, an engagement between the researcher and the 'researched' in which the creative power of social

---

[50] A. Appadurai (ed.) *The Social Life of Things: Commodities in Cultural Perspective* (Cambridge University Press, 1986); I. Kopytoff, 'The cultural biography of things: commoditization as process', in A. Appadurai, (ed.) *The Social Life of Things: Commodities in Cultural Perspective* (Cambridge University Press, 1986), pp. 64–94.

relations is realised and in which the ethnographer's commitment to radical cultural difference between researcher and researched is put at risk. What this means is that this will not be the kind of research which attempts to hide in the background but will, on the contrary, be research which involves both researcher and researched in the joint enactment of and deliberative engagement with ethics as a shared problem. It suggests, that is, a form of research which is itself implicated (explicitly) in the enactment of the moral as problematic, i.e. as *ethical*.[51] And this points to a particularly creative and productive use of reflexivity and of a singularly interesting form of research encounter for the enactment of ethics as an object of concern.[52]

The Genethics Club

The primary focus of this book has been a particular research experience of my own, the Genethics Club. In this concluding section – drawing upon the discussion in previous chapters – I want to offer a sketch of some of the ways in which the Genethics Club and, specifically, my participation in and analysis of it – exemplifies the potential for ethicoethnographic research of the type I have been discussing.

When the Genethics Club was established in 2001, our aim was to provide a space in which anyone working in clinical genetics – counsellors, doctors and laboratory staff – could present and discuss ethical issues arising in their practice and together work towards the development of shared models of good practice across the different regional genetics services. The model for this was the Dysmorphology Club, a pre-existing regular national forum for the presentation and discussion of difficult *clinical* cases by members of the twenty-three different Regional Genetics Services. Meetings of the Genethics Club take the form of a series of presentations by genetics professionals of cases that they or their colleagues consider to raise ethical problems. These case presentations and the free-flowing and open discussion by which they are followed have often been very rich, opening up practice and generating many further issues, different to those initially presented for

---

[51] G.E. Marcus, 'The uses of complicity in the changing mis-en-scène of anthropological fieldwork' in G.E. Marcus (ed.) *Ethnography Through Thick and Thin* (Princeton University Press, 1998), pp. 105–132.

[52] M. Fortun, 'Experiments in ethnography and its performance' (posted on Mannvernd website, 2000) available at www.mannvernd.is/english/articles/mfortun.html (accessed 9 February 2007); K. Fortun and M. Fortun, 'Scientific imaginaries and ethical plateaus in contemporary U.S. toxicology' (2005) 107 *American Anthropologist*, 1, 43–54.

discussion. I have attempted to capture some of the flavour of this in the analysis of cases in the earlier chapters of this book.

The ethicist's role in the Genethics Club – my role – has been multi-faceted.[53] Perhaps most importantly, I have been responsible for the continued maintenance of the Genethics Club as a welcoming social space across multiple genetics practices in a number of different locations. I have organised the space to allow sufficient time for the presentation of the cases. I have facilitated the subsequent discussion, ensuring that all who want to speak have a chance to do so. I have tried to ensure that marginal voices and perspectives are heard and taken seriously. I have used my knowledge of the literature, my experience of previous Genethics Club meetings and my experience of work in a genetics unit, to introduce issues and contrasting practices I think have been overlooked. I have adopted a methodologically critical stance to established practices. In other words, I have implicated myself – and been *complicit* – in the enactment of everyday, relatively stable moral practices and commitments as ethical problems. At the same time, I have observed and attempted to track ethical problems as they have emerged and changed over the course of a meeting, and over the life of the Genethics Club, bearing in mind that my role is deeply implicated in the enactment of ethics in this setting.[54] This has involved making notes of connections between discussions, reading and re-reading notes of cases and discussions from previous meetings, making connections between different cases, giving presentations to the Genethics Club about emerging themes, and encouraging the genetics professionals who present cases to report back about the 'outcome' or the ongoing trajectory of the ethical problems they have encountered.

I want now, finally, to conclude by commenting briefly on some of the features of ethics as it has been enacted in the Genethics Club, identifying as I do this some additional cross-cutting connections between the different chapters in this book.

One of the things that has been a persistent and recurring theme throughout the discussions at the Genethics Club is the way in which the problematisation by everyday practices of the relatively stable moral commitments of genetics professionals has often been linked to the spatial and/or temporal distribution of material objects. While, in an

---

[53] In this section, because my focus is on an analysis of the role of the 'ethicist', I am focusing on my own role. The Genethics Club is, however, organised and run jointly by Tara Clancy, Angus Clarke, Anneke Lucassen and myself and the origins and development of the Genethics Club are described in Chapter 1.

[54] The Genethics Club has also resulted in a number of publications in peer-reviewed journals. A list of these is available at www.genethicsclub.org.

unproblematised situation, material objects are seamlessly woven into everyday practice – family pedigrees are produced, blood samples are taken, medical records are filed away, and so on – in some cases the movement of these material objects into different physical locations, or the changing particularity of their arrangement or configuration, can create ethical problems. An example of this was provided by the exploration in Chapter 2 of the ways in which ethical problems can be created by the construction and verification of the family pedigree – through which the 'family' is transformed into a complex and changing assemblage of 'families' and the commitment to the patient in the family becomes a commitment to the patient in the 'families'. This transformation of the family through the movement and bringing together of different material objects into the family file can create difficulties for the genetics professional committed to the care of the 'patient in the family' as different parts of the 'families' in the pedigree are illuminated and become relevant or irrelevant in different spaces and at different times.

This can happen, for example, in situations where the bringing together of several pedigrees in a single master pedigree produces information relevant to the care or life choices of an individual who has not asked for it, and who was not aware that the 'validation' of the pedigree was taking place. In these situations, the construction of the master pedigree has created ethical problems around the moral commitment of the genetics professional to the family and around the use and storage of medical information.[55] In other words, the transformation of a previously unproblematic moral practice into an object of ethical concern is bound up with the spatial arrangement and movement of material objects. In this context, it is not difficult to see that the movement of a biological sample or medical record from the clinic to the laboratory, or across an international border, can have the potential to transform the patient in the families dramatically, and for the number of possible ethical objects of concern to multiply. Several cases of this type were discussed in earlier chapters. By the exploration of such cases, the Genethics Club serves to enrich everyone's understanding of ethics as an object of concern in their practice. Importantly, it does this not by complementing ethical deliberation with empirical richness, but through the enfolding of the ethical and the moral: the analysis shows how ethics is an assemblage constituted by the organisation of material

---

[55] M. Parker and A. Lucassen, 'Genetic information: a joint account?' (2004) 329 *British Medical Journal*, 165–167.

objects and everyday practices in specific spatial and temporal relations in which some things change and others remain the same.

By contrast, in some cases a particular configuration of materials and practices gives rise to an ethical object of concern that is *already* multiple. A particularly good example of this is a frequently occurring case presented at the Genethics Club in which a genetic test requested by one patient has the potential to reveal the genetic status of one of their relatives with the same degree of certainty as would a test on the relative themselves. Several such cases were discussed in Chapters 2 and 5. This might happen, for instance, where one twin wishes to take a presymptomatic test for breast cancer but the other, who is genetically identical, either does not wish to have their status revealed, or simply does not know that the test is being considered. On some occasions these cases are presented by genetics professionals at the Genethics Club as an ethical problem on account of the issues of consent and counselling. Here, genetics professionals see the case as problematic both because a test on one twin will reveal the genetic status of the other (who has not given consent), and also because there is the potential for this twin to be informed of their genetic status without having received appropriate counselling and support. On other occasions, or from the perspective of a different set of genetics professionals, this type of case is presented as an ethical problem on account of the issue of duty of care to the patient in front of them. This is because, were it to be decided that the provision of the test ought to depend upon the consent of both twins, for example in cases where the second twin is demanding that the test should not go ahead, this would in effect be to provide a third party – with whom the doctor may or may not also be in contact – with an unacceptable veto over the provision of care to the patient.[56] The enactment of this object of ethical concern from the perspective of two different sets of practitioners – and sometimes by the same genetics professional at different times – gives rise to ethics as a multiple object of concern, the multiplicity of which in this case cannot be resolved.[57]

The multiplicity of ethics exemplified by the case above and by the cases discussed in Chapter 5 means that the Genethics Club, as a space which brings together different health professionals – geneticists, counsellors and laboratory staff – from a wide range of locations, is inevitably and frequently characterised by the juxtaposition of diverse

---

[56] M. Parker and A. Lucassen, 'Concern for individuals and families in clinical genetics' (2003) 29 *Journal of Medical Ethics*, 70–73.

[57] A. Mol, *The Body Multiple: Ontology in Medical Practice* (Durham: Duke University Press, 2002).

ethical practices. The presentation and discussion of cases – such as the one above – shows them to be ethically problematic in different ways in different locations. One of the things that has become apparent as an ongoing theme in the Genethics Club is that the multiplicity of ethics, combined with awareness of the possibility of the movement of patients, samples and even genetics professionals between settings can sometimes lead to the enactment of this multiplicity itself as problematic. Here, the Genethics Club provides a space within which everyday moral commitments and the practices associated with them in different places or different communities of practice can be problematised – brought into existence as an object of ethical concern – by the juxtaposition of divergent practices, and by the defamiliarisation which this brings about. In the case of the twins described above, for example, the presentation of practice as problematic in one setting in a different way to the way it is understood as problematic in another *itself* comes to be seen as problematic – as an ethical object of concern. The awareness, in the Genethics Club, that patients in one setting may gain access to tests not available elsewhere, or that patients in one area, but not in another (who may well be members of the same family), may be 'tested' without their consent, has problematised practice in ways which raise important ethical questions about the configuration of genetic services locally, nationally and even internationally. This may lead those present to make attempts to justify the maintenance of diversity of practice between different clinics, that is, to preserve difference, or to engage in efforts to reach agreement about which shared practice should be adopted from now on across different settings. In either case, such deliberations will inevitably need to call upon ethical objects capable of moving across boundaries between practices – between different clinics, for example, or between the clinic and the laboratory – and this is likely to involve engagement with thick ethical objects such as 'justice', 'fairness', 'duties of care' and so on in something like the ways I discussed earlier in this chapter.

A related ongoing theme emerging from the Genethics Club is that, once raised in relation to a particular case, such ethical objects can go on to put unproblematised practice and difference elsewhere at risk, for example, when genetics professionals go back to their teams and engage in discussion about practices in other clinics, exerting an influence well beyond the case under consideration. This makes possible another way in which the Genethics Club serves to enrich understanding of ethics as an object of concern in genetics – through the deliberative exploration (elsewhere) of the relationships between these moving objects – justice, fairness, duties of care and so on – and previously unproblematic practice. In such explorations, mobile ethical objects of concern are themselves put at risk and the creative power of social relations provides an opportunity for practice to be opened up, for new practices to emerge, and for new kinds of encounters with experience to be made. They provide, that is, opportunities for the exercise and development of *moral craftsmanship*.

Glossary of medical terms

This is a brief glossary of the key medical terms used in the text. My aim in putting this glossary together has been to provide some additional information relevant to the reading of the cases discussed in the book rather than to provide a very detailed or comprehensive explanation of the various terms.[1]

Alport Syndrome

Alport Sydrome is a condition the symptoms of which can include renal failure, deafness and eye problems. The pattern of inheritance can be X-linked, autosomal recessive or autosomal dominant but the majority of families follow an X-linked form. The average age of onset, for the X-linked form, is in the mid-twenties. Prenatal testing through chorionic villus sampling (CVS) is possible if the disease-causing mutation in the family is known. Carriers and at-risk family members should be monitored through regular appointments with a nephrologist.

Inherited breast cancer (BRCA1 and BRCA2)

BRCA1 and BRCA2 are both dominantly inherited large genes with many possible disease-causing mutations scattered throughout the gene. Female carriers of a mutation in BRCA1 have an average lifetime risk of breast cancer of between 44 per cent and 78 per cent and a risk of ovarian cancer of between 18 per cent and 54 per cent. Female carriers of BRCA2 are at an average lifetime risk of breast cancer of 45 per cent and of 11 per cent of ovarian cancer. Male carriers of BRCA1 and, particularly, BRCA2 are also at increased risk of breast cancer and other cancers including prostate cancer. Interventions include regular screening

---

[1] The information in this glossary draws heavily on that in H.V. Firth and J.A. Hurst, *Oxford Desk Reference Clinical Genetics* (Oxford University Press, 2005). This is an excellent source of additional information.

(mammography (from 50–65), ultrasound (often for younger women, less than 30), MRI and breast examination) and/or prophylactic mastectomy or oophorectomy.

Charcot-Marie-Tooth (CMT)

Charcot-Marie-Tooth is a disease involving difficulty walking, progressive foot deformity and gradual loss of muscle strength and bulk in lower legs and sometimes in hands. CMT usually presents in children between 5 and 15. There is a wide range of severity. Some gene carriers (about 10 per cent) will be asymptomatic throughout their lives. A small number will be more severely affected and have significantly impaired mobility. Prenatal diagnosis is available for CMT if the mutation in the family is known but this is rarely requested.

Chorionic villus sampling (CVS)

CVS is a form of prenatal testing which involves testing samples of the developing placenta (chorion) from between 11 and 13 weeks of gestation. CVS has a risk of miscarriage of between 1.5 and 2 per cent.

Cystic fibrosis (CF)

Cystic fibrosis is an autosomal recessive condition leading, primarily, to chronic pulmonary disease. The age of onset and rate of progression of pulmonary disease are very variable. Current median survival is late twenties or early thirties and survival to the thirties and forties is no longer rare. Most men with CF are infertile, and fertility in women is reduced. Prenatal testing (CVS) is available from 11 weeks gestation.

Duchenne muscular dystrophy (DMD)

DMD is an X-linked recessive disorder primarily affecting males. It is characterised by progressive muscle wasting and boys with DMD will become wheelchair dependent from between 7 and 13 years of age and currently die in their late teens or early twenties. Some female carriers of a DMD mutation will manifest some symptoms. Prenatal testing is available using CVS from 11 weeks gestation if the disease-causing mutation in the family is known.

Dysmorphology

Dysmorphology is the recognition and study of birth defects and syndromes. In the context of the cases discussed in this book, the use of the term tends to indicate a contrast between the use of clinical skills to identify conditions and the use of diagnostic genetic testing (whether molecular or cytogenetic).

Edwards' Syndrome (Trisomy 18)

Babies with Edwards' Syndrome have an additional copy of chromosome 18. These babies tend to be small and have congenital heart defects. They generally have a very short life expectancy – the median life expectancy is four days – but there are very exceptional cases of longer-term survival. The majority of cases of Edwards' Syndrome are due to *de novo* mutations, i.e. mutations not present in the parents.

Familial adenomatous polyposis coli (FAP)

Familial adenomatous polyposis coli (FAP) is a dominantly inherited colorectal cancer predisposing syndrome. Screening (colonoscopy) is available from the early teens.

Fragile X

Fragile X Syndrome (FRAX) is a common X-linked cause of inherited mental retardation in males – the average IQ of males with a full mutation is around 40. Affected males tend to have developmental delay and some degree of speech and language impairment – this can be variable ranging from a complete absence of speech through to very mild communication difficulties. Female carriers of the full mutation are much less affected than males because they have another X-chromosome. However, approximately 50 per cent of females with a full mutation will have some learning and behavioural difficulties.

Haemochromatosis

Hereditary haemochromatosis type 1 is an autosomal recessive disorder of iron metabolism. Males are often more affected than females. Age of onset is in the mid to late forties. The penetrance of the disorder is low and its expression is variable. For those who are affected, treatment includes the taking of blood (venesection) two to four times a year. If patients are diagnosed early, and they are treated with venesection, life expectancy is normal.

Hereditary non-polyposis coli (HNPCC)

Hereditary non-polyposis coli (HNPCC) or 'Lynch Syndrome' is a dominantly inherited syndrome predisposing people to colon cancer. Screening is available in late teens and early twenties.

Huntington's Disease (HD)

Huntington's Disease is a progressive, untreatable, neurological disorder involving involuntary movements, dementia and psychiatric disturbance. Age of onset is different in different families, but generally speaking, the peak age of onset of symptoms is between 40 and 45. Earlier and later onset is possible. Inheritance of Huntington's Disease is autosomal dominant.

Kleinfelter Syndrome (47XXY)

Kleinfelter Syndrome is generally detected during prenatal testing as an incidental finding or in adult life during investigations for male infertility. Males with Kleinfelter's Syndrome have a normal lifespan and most are probably never diagnosed. 47XXY men enter puberty normally and their sexual relations are unaffected but they are usually infertile.

Li-Fraumeni Syndrome

Li-Fraumeni Syndrome is a rare autosomal dominant condition. The cancer risk in TP53 mutation carriers (the most common form of Li-Fraumeni mutation) is around 70 per cent for males and nearly 100 per cent for females. Prenatal testing via CVS from 11 weeks is possible if the familial mutation is known.

Lynch Syndrome

See HNPCC above.

Marfan Syndrome

Marfan Syndrome is an autosomal dominantly inherited disorder of the connective tissue. Cardiovascular disease is the main cause of morbidity and mortality and if left untreated life expectancy can be reduced by

30–40 per cent. Marfan Syndrome is associated with a number of dys-morphic features including above-average height and long limbs such as disproportionately long arms and fingers.

Myotonic dystrophy

Myotonic dystrophy is a common autosomal dominantly inherited neuromuscular disorder. The age of onset is between 20 and 30 years. The condition is very variable and its progression is difficult to predict. Life expectancy is around 60 years. The condition is char-acterised by muscle weakness and difficulties with mobility, fertil-ity problems and gastrointenstinal conditions such as irritable bowel syndrome.

Neurofribromatosis Type 1 (NF1)

NF1 is an autosomal dominantly inherited disorder which leads to 'café-au-lait' skin spots, and neurofibromas – benign tumours of the peripheral nervous system. NF1 is fully penetrant but very variably expressed and difficult to predict. However, there is a risk of serious complications throughout life, hence regular life-long surveillance is required. Lifespan is reduced with a mean age of death of around fifty.

Prader-Willi Syndrome

Prader-Willi Syndrome is a condition caused by deletions or deactiva-tion on chromosome 15. Most patients with Prader-Willi Syndrome have an IQ in the 60s and most adults with the condition will need sup-port in adult life and will not live independently. Typically patients with Prader-Willi Syndrome have an insatiable appetite and obesity.

Preimplantation genetic diagnosis (PGD)

Preimplantation genetic diagnosis uses in-vitro fertilisation techniques to obtain fertilised embryos. Twelve cells are removed for genetic ana-lysis from several embryos at the 816-cell stage. Only embryos in which genetic testing predicts that the developing embryos will not develop the genetic disorder are implanted in the mother.

Retinoschisis

Inherited retinoschisis is an X-linked disorder affecting the vision of males. The effect on eyesight can vary. Very few men with the condition will lose their sight completely but some will have very limited reading vision. In many cases carriers of retinoschisis will be asymptomatic.

Spinal muscular atrophy (SMA)

Spinal muscular atrophy is an autosomal recessive condition causing muscle weakness. There is a spectrum of clinical severity. In SMA type 1, the onset of muscle weakness is in the first few months of life and can be severe leading to fatal respiratory failure in the first six months of life or up to two years. In SMA type 2, the onset of muscle weakness is before eighteen months. The child will be able to sit but unable to walk unaided. However, survival into adult life is usual.

X-linked disorders

X-linked disorders are caused by mutations on the X chromosome. They can be dominant or recessive. Males with dominant X-linked conditions are severely affected. Female carriers are affected but less severely than males. Males with recessive X-linked conditions (such as Duchenne muscular dystrophy) are also severely affected. Female carriers are unaffected or more mildly affected. When a father with an X-linked condition has a child, all of his daughters will be carriers (because they will have inherited one of their X-chromosomes from him) and none of his sons will be affected (because they will have inherited their X-chromosome from their mother).

Bibliography

Appadurai, A. 'Introduction: commodities and the politics of value', in A. Appadurai (ed.) *The Social Life of Things: Commodities in Cultural Perspective* (Cambridge University Press, 1986), pp. 3–63

Modernity at Large (Minneapolis: University of Minnesota Press, 1996)

(ed.) *The Social Life of Things: Commodities in Cultural Perspective* (Cambridge University Press, 1986)

Appelbaum, P.S. and Roth, L.H. 'The therapeutic misconception: informed consent in psychiatric research' (1982) 5 *International Journal of Law and Psychiatry*, 319–329

Aristotle, *Nicomachean Ethics* (London: Penguin, 1976)

Armstrong, D., Michie, S. and Marteau, T. 'Revealed identity: a study of the process of genetic counselling' (1998) 47 *Social Science and Medicine*, 11, 1653–1658

Ashcroft, R.E. 'Ethical issues in statistical genetics', in D.J. Balding, M.J. Bishop and C. Cannings (eds.) *Handbook of Statistical Genetics*, third edition (Chichester: John Wiley and Sons, 2007), pp. 1325–1345

Ashcroft, R.E., Lucassen, A., Parker, M., Widdershoven, G. and Verkerk, M. (eds.) *Case Analysis in Clinical Ethics* (Cambridge University Press, 2005)

Bosk, C. *All God's Mistakes: Genetic Counseling in a Pediatric Hospital* (University of Chicago Press, 1992)

'Irony, ethnography, and informed consent', in B. Hoffmaster (ed.) *Bioethics in Social Context* (Philadelphia: Temple University Press, 2001), pp. 199–220

'Professional ethicist available: logical, secular, friendly' (1999) 128 *Daedalus*, 47–68

What Would You Do? Juggling Bioethics and Ethnography (University of Chicago Press, 2008)

Boulton, M. and Parker, M. 'Informed consent in a changing environment' (2007) 65 *Social Science and Medicine*, 2187–2198

Bradley-Smith, G., Hope, S., Firth, H.V. and Hurst, J.A. *Oxford Handbook of Genetics* (Oxford University Press, 2010)

British Society for Human Genetics *Genetic Testing of Children* (Birmingham: British Society for Human Genetics, 2010) available at www.bshg.org.uk/GTOC_2010_BSHG.pdf (accessed 1 August 2011)

Brown, N., Rappert, B. and Webster, A. 'Introducing contested futures: from looking into the future to looking at the future', in N. Brown, N. Rappert and A. Webster, *Contested Futures: A Sociology of Prospective Technoscience* (Aldershot: Ashgate, 2000), pp. 3–20

Burke, B. and Kolker, A. 'Directiveness in prenatal genetics counselling' (1994) 22 *Women and Health*, 31–53

Burke, S., Bennett, C., Bedward, J. and Fardon, P. *The Experiences and Preferences of People Receiving Genetic Information from Healthcare Professionals* (Birmingham: NHS National Genetics Education and Development Centre, 2007)

Caplan, A. 'Neutrality is not morality: the ethics of genetic counseling', in A. Caplan, B. LeRoy and D. Bartels (eds.) *Prescribing our Future: Ethical Challenges in Genetic Counseling* (New York: Aldine Press, 1993), pp. 149–165

Carson, R.A. 'Interpretive bioethics: the way of discernment' (1990) 11 *Theoretical Medicine and Bioethics*, 51–60

Chadwick, R. 'Genetics, choice and responsibility' (1999) 1 *Health, Risk and Society*, 293–300

Clarke, A. *Genetic Counselling: Practice and Principles* (London: Routledge, 1994)

'Outcomes and process in genetic counselling', in P. Harper and A. Clarke, *Genetics, Society and Clinical Practice* (Oxford: Bios Scientific Publishing, 1997), pp. 165–178

'The process of genetic counselling: beyond nondirectiveness', in P. Harper and A. Clarke, *Genetics, Society and Clinical Practice* (Oxford: Bios Scientific Publishing, 1997), pp. 179–200

Clarke, A., Richards, M., Kerzin-Storrar, L., *et al.*, 'Genetic professionals' reports of nondisclosure of genetic risk information within families' (2005) 13 *European Journal of Human Genetics*, 556–562

Clinical Genetics Society, *Guidelines for Pedigree Drawing* (Birmingham: Clinical Genetics Society, 2001) available at www.clingensoc.org/Docs/Standards/CGSPedigree.pdf (accessed 29 July 2011)

Cunningham-Burley, S. and Kerr, A. 'Defining the "social": towards an understanding of scientific and medical discourses on the social aspects of the new genetics' (1999) 21 *Sociology of Health and Illness*, 647–668

D'Agincourt-Canning, L. 'Experiences of genetic risk: disclosure and the gendering of responsibility' (2001) 15 *Bioethics*, 3, 231–247

Davis, D.S. *Genetic Dilemmas: Reproductive Technology, Parental Choices and Children's Futures* (New York: Routledge, 2001)

'Rich cases: the ethics of thick description' (1991) 21 *Hastings Center Report*, 4, 12–17

de Vries, R.G. 'Toward a sociology of bioethics' (1995) 18 *Qualitative Sociology*, 1, 119–128

Dewey, J. *Human Nature and Conduct* (New York: Prometheus Books, 2002)

Dixon-Woods, M. 'Why is patient safety so hard? A selective review of ethnographic studies' (2010) 15 (Suppl. 1) *Journal of Health Services Research and Policy*, 11–16

Dolgin, J. 'Choice, tradition, and the new genetics: the fragmentation of the ideology of family' (2000) 32 *Connecticut Law Review*, 523–566

Dunn, M., Sheehan, M., Hope, T. and Parker, M. 'Towards methodological innovation in empirical ethics research' (in press) *Cambridge Quarterly of Healthcare Ethics*

Dzur, A. 'Democratizing the hospital: deliberative-democratic bioethics' (2002) 27 *Journal of Health Politics, Policy and Law*, 2, 177–211

Edwards, J. *Born and Bred: Idioms of Kinship and New Reproductive Technologies in England* (Oxford University Press, 2000)

Faden, R. and Beauchamp, T. *A History and Theory of Informed Consent* (Oxford University Press, 1986)

Featherstone, K., Atkinson, P., Bharadwaj, A. and Clarke, A. *Risky Relations: Family, Kinship and the New Genetics* (Oxford: Berg, 2006)

Finkler, K. *Experiencing the New Genetics: Family and Kinship on the Medical Frontier* (Philadelphia: University of Pennsylvania Press, 2000)

Firth, H.V. and Hurst, J.A. *Oxford Desk Reference: Clinical Genetics* (Oxford University Press, 2005)

Fluehr-Lobban, C. *Ethics and the Profession of Anthropology: Dialogue for Ethically Conscious Practice*, second edition (Walnut Creek: AltaMira Press, 2003)

'Globalization of research and international standards of ethics in anthropology' (2000) 925 *Annals of the New York Academy of Sciences*, 37–44

Fortun, K. and Fortun, M. 'Scientific imaginaries and ethical plateaus in contemporary U.S. toxicology' (2005) 107 *American Anthropologist*, 1, 43–54

Fortun, M. 'Experiments in ethnography and its performance' (posted on Mannvernd website, 2000) available at www.mannvernd.is/english/articles/mfortun.html (accessed 9 February 2007)

Fox, R.C. 'Advanced medical technology – social and ethical implications' (1976) 2 *Annual Review of Sociology*, 231–268

'Observations and reflections of a perpetual fieldworker' (2004) 595 *Annals of the American Academy*, 309–326

Fox, R.C. and Swazey, J.P. 'Examining American bioethics: its problems and prospects' (2005) 14 *Cambridge Quarterly of Healthcare Ethics*, 361–373

Observing Bioethics (Oxford University Press, 2008)

Franklin, S. 'Re-thinking nature-culture: anthropology and the new genetics' (2003) 3 *Anthropological Theory*, 1, 65–85

Franklin, S. and McKinnon, S. 'Relative values: reconfiguring kinship studies', in S. Franklin and S. McKinnon (eds.) *Relative Values: Reconfiguring Kinship Studies* (Durham and London: Duke University Press, 2001), pp. 1–25

Freidson, F. *Profession of Medicine: A Sociology of Applied Knowledge* (University of Chicago Press, 1988)

Geertz, C. *The Interpretation of Cultures* (New York: Basic Books, 1973)

General Medical Council, *Confidentiality* (London: General Medical Council, 2009)

Good Medical Practice (London: General Medical Council, 2006)

Gieryn, T.F. 'Boundary-work and the demarcation of science from non-science: strains and interests in professional ideologies of scientists' (1983) 48 *American Sociological Review*, 6, 781–795

Glover, J. *Causing Death and Saving Lives* (London: Penguin Books, 1977)

Goethe, J.W. Von, *Elective Affinities* (London: Penguin Books, 1971 [1809])

Hallowell, N. 'Doing the right thing: genetic risk and responsibility' (1999) 21 *Sociology of Health and Illness*, 5, 597–621

Hallowell, N., Cooke, S., Crawford, G., Lucassen, A. and Parker, M. 'Distinguishing research from clinical care in cancer genetics: theoretical justifications and practical strategies' (2009) 68 *Social Science and Medicine*, 2010–2017

Hallowell, N., Cooke, S., Crawford, G., Parker, M. and Lucassen, A. 'Defining research and clinical care: health care professionals' and researchers' understanding of cancer genetics activities' (2009) 35 *Journal of Medical Ethics*, 113–119

Hammersley, M. and Atkinson, P. *Ethnography: Principles in Practice* (London: Routledge, 2006)

Harper, P. *Practical Genetic Counselling*, sixth edition (London: Edward Arnold, 2004)

A Short History of Medical Genetics (Oxford University Press, 2008)

Hoeyer, K. ' "Ethics wars": reflections on the antagonism between bioethicists and social science observers of biomedicine' (2006) 29 *Human Studies*, 203–227

Hoffmaster, B. (ed.) *Bioethics in Social Context* (Philadelphia: Temple University Press, 2001)

Hoffmaster, B. 'Can ethnography save the life of medical ethics?' (1992) 35 *Social Science and Medicine*, 12, 1421–1432

Hoffmaster, B. and Hooker, C. 'How experience confronts ethics' (2009) 23 *Bioethics*, 4, 214–225

Hope, A. 'Empirical medical ethics' (1999) *Journal of Medical Ethics*, 219–220

Human Genetics Commission, *Inside Information: Balancing Interests in the Use of Personal Data* (London: UK Department of Health, 2002)

Making Babies: Reproductive Decisions and Genetic Technologies (London: UK Department of Health, 2006)

Jennings, B. (1990) 'Ethics and ethnography in neonatal intensive care', in G. Weisz (ed.) *Social Science Perspectives on Medical Ethics* (Philadelphia: University of Pennsylvania Press, 1990), pp. 261–272

Joint Committee on Medical Genetics, *Consent and Confidentiality in Genetic Practice: Guidance on Genetic Testing and Sharing Genetic Information* (London: Royal College of Physicians of London, 2006)

Katz, J. *The Silent World of Doctor and Patient* (New York: Free Press, 1984)

Katz-Rothman, B. *The Tentative Pregnancy* (New York: W.W. Norton and Company, 1986)

Kee, F., Tiret, L., Robo, J.Y., Nicaud, V., McCrum, E., Evans, A. and Cambien, F. 'Reliability of reported family history of myocardial infarction' (1993) 307 *British Medical Journal*, 6918, 1528–1530

Kerr, A. and Cunningham-Burley, S. 'On ambivalence and risk: reflexive modernity and the new human genetics' (2000) 34 *Sociology*, 2, 283–304

Kerr, A., Cunningham-Burley, S. and Amos, A. 'Eugenics and the new genetics in Britain: examining contemporary professionals' accounts' (1998) 23 *Science, Technology and Human Values*, 2, 175–198

'The new genetics: professionals' discursive boundaries' (1997) 45 *The Sociological Review*, 2, 279–303

Kleinman, A. 'Moral experience and ethical reflection: can ethnography reconcile them? A quandary for "the new bioethics" ' (1999) 128 *Daedalus*, 4, 69–97

Writing at the Margin: Discourse Between Anthropology and Medicine (Berkeley: University of California Press, 1997)

Kon, A.A. 'The role of empirical research in bioethics' (2009) 6 *American Journal of Bioethics*, 3, 59–65

Konrad, M. *Narrating the New Predictive Genetics* (Cambridge University Press, 2005)

Kopytoff, I. 'The cultural biography of things: commoditization as process', in A. Appadurai (ed.) *The Social Life of Things: Commodities in Cultural Perspective* (Cambridge University Press, 1986), pp. 64–94

Law, J. and Urry, J. 'Enacting the social' (2004) 33 *Economy and Society*, 3, 390–410

Lippman, A. 'The genetic construction of prenatal testing: choice, consent or conformity for women?', in K. Rothenberg and F. Thomsen (eds.) *Women and Prenatal Testing* (Ohio State University Press, 1991), pp. 9–34

'Led (astray) by genetic maps: the cartography of the human genome and health care' (1992) 35 *Social Science and Medicine*, 12, 1469–1476

Lucassen, A. and Parker, M. 'Revealing false paternity: some ethical considerations' (2001) 357 *The Lancet*, 1033–1035

Lucassen, A., Wheeler, R. and Parker, M. 'Implications of data protection legislation for family history' (2006) 332 *British Medical Journal*, 299–301

Mandelbaum, M. *Phenomenology of Moral Experience* (Baltimore: Johns Hopkins Press, 1969)

Marcus, G.E. 'The uses of complicity in the changing mis-en-scène of anthropological fieldwork' in G.E. Marcus (ed.) *Ethnography Through Thick and Thin* (Princeton University Press, 1998), pp. 105–132

Marcus, G.E. and Fischer, M.M.J. *Anthropology as Cultural Critique: An Experimental Moment in the Human Sciences* (University of Chicago Press, 1986)

Marshall, P.A. 'Anthropology and bioethics' (1992) 6 *Medical Anthropology Quarterly*, 1, 49–73

Marteau, T. and Drake, H. 'Attributions for disability: the influence of genetic screening' (1995) 40 *Social Science and Medicine*, 1127–1132

Marteau, T., Drake, H. and Bobrow, M. 'Counselling following diagnosis of a foetal abnormality: the differing approaches of obstetricians, clinical geneticists and genetic nurses' (1994) 31 *Journal of Medical Genetics*, 864–867

McMillan, J. and Hope, A. 'The possibility of empirical psychiatric ethics', in G. Widdershoven, T. Hope, J. McMillan and L. van der Scheer (eds.) *Empirical Ethics in Psychiatry* (Oxford University Press, 2008), pp. 9–22

Meskell, L. and Pels, P. (eds.) *Embedding Ethics* (Oxford: Berg, 2005)

Michaels, M. and Morgan, L. 'Introduction: the fetal imperative', in L. Morgan and M. Michaels (eds.) *Fetal Subjects, Feminist Positions* (Philadelphia: University of Pennsylvania Press, 1999), pp. 1–10

Mol, A. *The Body Multiple: Ontology in Medical Practice* (Durham: Duke University Press, 2002)

Muller, J.H. 'Anthropology, bioethics and medicine: a provocative trilogy' (1994) 8 *Medical Anthropology Quarterly*, 4, 448–467

Murphy, E. and Dingwall, R. 'Informed consent, anticipatory regulation and ethnographic practice' (2007) 65 *Social Science and Medicine*, 11, 2223–2234

Newson, A.J. and Humphries, S.E. 'Cascade testing in familial hypercholesterolaemia: how should family members be contacted?' (2005) 13 *European Journal of Human Genetics*, 401–408

NHS National Genetics Education and Development Centre, *Taking and Drawing a Family History* (Birmingham: NHS National Genetics Education and Development Centre, 2008)

Novas, C. 'Genetic advocacy groups, science and biovalue: creating political economies of hope', in P. Atkinson, P. Glasner and H. Greenslade (eds.) *New Genetics, New Identities* (London: Routledge, 2006), pp. 11–27

Novas, C. and Rose, N. 'Genetic risk and the birth of the somatic individual' (2000) 29 *Economy and Society*, 4, 485–513

Nugaka, Y. and Cambrosio, A. 'Medical pedigrees and the visual production of family disease in Canadian and Japanese genetic counselling practice', in M.A. Elston (ed.) *The Sociology of Medical Science and Technology* (Oxford: Blackwell, 1997), pp. 29–56

Parens, E. and Asch, A. 'The disability rights critique of prenatal testing: reflections and recommendations' (2003) 9 *Mental Retardation and Developmental Disabilities Research Reviews*, 1, 40–47

Parker, M. 'Children who run: ethics and homelessness', in B. Almond, *Introducing Applied Ethics* (Oxford: Blackwell, 1995), pp. 58–70
  'Deliberative bioethics', in R.E. Ashcroft, A. Dawson, H. Draper and J. McMillan (eds.) *Principles of Health Care Ethics*, second edition (Chichester: John Wiley and Sons, 2007), pp. 185–191
  'Ethnography/ethics' (2007) 65 *Social Science and Medicine*, 2248–2259
  'Genetic testing in children and young people' (2009) 9 *Familial Cancer*, 1, 15–18

Parker, M., Ashcroft, R., Wilkie, A. and Kent, A. 'Ethical review of research into rare genetic disorders' (2004) 329 *British Medical Journal*, 288–289

Parker, M. and Dickenson, D. *The Cambridge Medical Ethics Workbook* (Cambridge University Press, 2001)

Parker, M. and Lucassen, A. 'Concern for individuals and families in clinical genetics' (2003) 29 *Journal of Medical Ethics*, 70–73
  'Genetic information: a joint account?' (2004) 329 *British Medical Journal*, 165–167

Parker, M., Williamson, R. and Savulescu, J. *Ethical Issues in Genetics Research: An Introduction for Members of Australian Human Research Ethics Committees* (Melbourne: Cooperative Research Centre for the Discovery of Genes for Common Human Diseases, 2003)

Pels, P. 'Professions of duplexity: a prehistory of ethical codes in anthropology' (1999) 40 *Current Anthropology*, 2, 101–136

'The trickster's dilemma: ethics and the technologies of the anthropological self', in M. Strathern (ed.) *Audit Culture: Anthropological Studies in Accountability, Ethics, and the Academy* (London: Routledge, 2000), pp. 135–172

' "Where there aren't no ten commandments": redefining ethics during the Darkness in El Dorado scandal', in L. Meskell and P. Pels (eds.) *Embedding Ethics* (Oxford: Berg, 2005), pp. 69–99

PFG Foundation, *Genetics and Mainstream Medicine: Service Development and Integration* (Cambridge: PFG Foundation, 2011)

Press, N. and Browner, C.H. 'Why women say yes to prenatal diagnosis' (1997) 45 *Social Science and Medicine*, 7, 979–989

Rapp, R. *Testing Women, Testing the Fetus: The Social Impact of Amniocentesis in America* (New York and London: Routledge, 2000)

Rapp, R., Heath, D. and Taussig, K. 'Genealogical disease: where heredity, abnormality, biomedical explanation, and family responsibility meet', in S. Franklin and S. McKinnon (eds.) *Relative Values: Reconfiguring Kinship Studies* (Durham and London: Duke University Press, 2001), pp. 384–409

Reed, S.C. 'A short history of genetic counselling' (1971) 21 *Social Biology*, 4, 332–339

Rose, P. 'Taking a family history', in P. Rose and A. Lucassen, *Practical Genetics for Primary Care* (Oxford University Press, 1999), pp. 57–75

Ruskin, J. 'The Nature of Gothic', in J. Ruskin, *Unto this Last and Other Writings* (London: Penguin Books, 1997), pp. 77–110

Ryle, G. 'The thinking of thoughts: What is "le Penseur" doing?', in G. Ryle, *Collected Papers II: Collected Essays 1929–1968* (London: Hutchinson, 1971)

Scheper-Hughes, N. 'The primacy of the ethical: propositions for a militant anthropology' (1995) 36 *Current Anthropology*, 3, 409–440

Schneider, D. *Critique of the Study of Kinship* (Ann Arbor: University of Michigan Press, 1984)

'Kinship and biology', in A.J. Coale, L.A. Fallers, M. Levy, D. Schneider and S. Tomkins (eds.) *Aspects of the Analysis of Family Structure* (Princeton University Press, 1965), pp. 83–101

Sennett, R. *The Craftsman* (London: Penguin, 2008)

Shakespeare, T. 'Back to the future? New genetics and disabled people' (1995) 44 *Critical Social Policy*, 45, 22–35

Disability Rights and Wrongs (London: Routledge, 2006)

Shaw, A. 'Interpreting images: diagnostic skill in the genetics clinic' (2003) 9 *Journal of the Royal Anthropological Institute*, 1, 39–55

Kinship and Continuity: Pakistani Families in Britain (Amsterdam: Harwood Academic Publishers, 2000)

Shelton, W. 'Empirical bioethics: present and future possibilities' (2009) 9 *American Journal of Bioethics*, 6–7, 74–75

Stacey, M. 'The new genetics: a feminist view', in T. Marteau and M. Richards (eds.) *The Troubled Helix* (Cambridge University Press, 1996), pp. 331–349

Strathern, M. 'Accountability and ethnography', in M. Strathern (ed.) *Audit Culture: Anthropological Studies in Accountability, Ethics, and the Academy* (London: Routledge, 2000), pp. 279–304

After Nature: English Kinship in the Late Twentieth Century (Cambridge University Press, 1992)

Kinship, Law and the Unexpected: Relatives Are Always a Surprise (Cambridge University Press, 2005)

Turner, L. 'Anthropological and sociological critiques of bioethics' (2009) 6 *Bioethical Inquiry*, 83–98

van der Scheer, L. and Widdershoven, G. 'Integrated empirical ethics: loss of normativity?' (2004) 7 *Medicine, Health Care and Philosophy*, 71–79

Vaughan, D. 'The dark side of organizations: mistake, misconduct, and disaster' (1999) 25 *Annual Review of Sociology*, 271–305

Wachbroit, R. and Wasserman, D. 'Patient autonomy and value-neutrality in nondirective genetic counselling' (1995) 6 *Stanford Law and Policy Review*, 2, 103–111

Wertz, D.C., Fletcher, J.C. and Mulvihill, J.J. 'Medical geneticists confront ethical dilemmas: cross-cultural comparisons among 18 nations' (1990) 46 *American Journal of Human Genetics*, 1200–1213

Widdershoven, G., Abma, T. and Molewijk, B. 'Empirical ethics as dialogical practice' (2009) 23 *Bioethics*, 4, 236–248

Williams, B. *Ethics and the Limits of Philosophy* (London: Penguin Books, 2006)

Williams, C. 'Framing the fetus in medical work: rituals and practices' (2005) 60 *Social Science and Medicine*, 2085–2095

Williams, C., Alderson, P. and Farsides, B. 'Is nondirectiveness possible within the context of antenatal screening and testing?' (2002) 54 *Social Science and Medicine*, 339–347

'Too many choices? Hospital and community staff reflect on the future of prenatal testing' (2002) 55 *Social Science and Medicine*, 743–753

Yanagisako, S.J. and Collier, J.F. 'Toward a unified analysis of gender and kinship', in J.F. Collier and S.J. Yanagisako (eds.) *Gender and Kinship: Essays Toward a Unified Analysis* (Stanford University Press, 1987), pp. 14–50

Index